CAMPAIGN 288

TARANTO 1940

The Fleet Air Arm's precursor to Pearl Harbor

ANGUS KONSTAM

ILLUSTRATED BY PETER DENNIS

Series editor Marcus Cowper

OSPREY PUBLISHING
Bloomsbury Publishing Plc

PO Box 883, Oxford, OX1 9PL, UK
1385 Broadway, 5th Floor, New York, NY 10018, USA
Email: info@ospreypublishing.com

OSPREY is a trademark of Osprey Publishing, a division of
Bloomsbury Publishing Plc

© 2015 Osprey Publishing

First published in Great Britain in 2015 by Osprey Publishing

Transferred to digital print-on-demand in 2019

Printed and bound in Great Britain

A CIP catalogue record for this book is available from the British Library.

ISBN: 978 1 4728 0896 7
PDF e-book ISBN: 978 1 4728 0897 4
e-Pub ISBN: 978 1 4728 0898 1

Editorial by Ilios Publishing Ltd, Oxford, UK (www.iliospublishing.com)
Index by Alan Rutter
Typeset in Myriad Pro and Sabon
Maps by Bounford.com
3D bird's-eye views by The Black Spot
Battlescene illustrations by Peter Dennis
Originated by PDQ Media, Bungay, UK

The Woodland Trust
Osprey Publishing supports the Woodland Trust, the UK's leading woodland
conservation charity.

www.ospreypublishing.com
To find out more about our authors and books visit our website. Here you
will find extracts, author interviews, details of forthcoming events and the
option to sign-up for our newsletter.

AUTHOR'S NOTE

All images are from the Stratford Archive, Edinburgh.

ARTIST'S NOTE

Readers may care to note that the original paintings from which the color
plates in this book were prepared are available for private sale. The
Publishers retain all reproduction copyright whatsoever. All enquiries
should be addressed to:

Peter Dennis, Fieldhead, The Park, Mansfield, Notts, NG18 2AT, UK
Email: magie.h@ntlworld.com

The Publishers regret that they can enter into no correspondence upon this
matter.

CONTENTS

Mediterranean Theatre of Operations, 1940

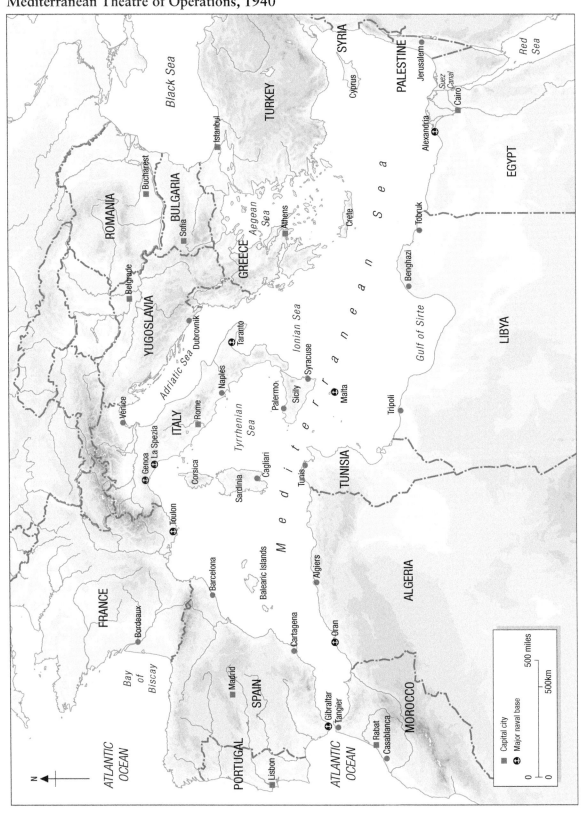

INTRODUCTION

In the Royal Navy, 21 October is celebrated as the anniversary of its greatest victory. That evening, both at sea and ashore, Trafalgar Night dinners are held, to commemorate the Battle of Trafalgar (1805), and the exploits of Horatio Nelson, arguably Britain's greatest admiral, who died at the moment of victory. However, in the Fleet Air Arm, while Trafalgar is still celebrated, the Royal Navy's aviators have their own victory to commemorate. So, in November each year, Taranto Night dinners are held to remember the exploits of the same evening three-quarters of a century ago. For the Fleet Air Arm, Taranto was a victory every bit as important as Trafalgar – the first great exploit by the youngest branch of the service.

Late in the evening of 11 November 1940, two groups of obsolete biplanes launched from a British aircraft carrier carried out a surprise attack on the Italian battle fleet, which was anchored in the southern Italian port of Taranto. The Italian ships were protected by antitorpedo nets, and screened by barrage balloons. Hundreds of anti-aircraft guns of various calibres ringed the ancient harbour, and listening devices – precursors of radar – were sited there, to provide early warning of an enemy air attack. Nearby, modern fighters of the Italian Air Force stood ready to defend the port against British bombers or torpedo planes, while search aircraft patrolled the skies to the south, looking for any British ships or aircraft foolhardy enough to come within range of the naval base. The admirals in charge of the fleet and the base considered Taranto to be virtually immune to air attack. Instead these impressive defences were tested, and found wanting.

The Royal Navy Historic Flight based in RNAS Yeovilton maintains and operates this Fairey Swordfish Mark II, one of two Swordfish still in flying condition. During the war it formed part of 836 Squadron, and was used in a convoy protection role in the North Atlantic. It is now a regular participant in British airshows.

Strangely, the 21 aircraft used in the attack were all lumbering Swordfish biplanes, aircraft which were already outdated when they entered service four years earlier. The Swordfish usually carried a crew of three, but for this raid one crewman – the rear gunner – was left behind, to make room for a long-range fuel tank. When carrying bombs or a torpedo it had a top speed of just over 140mph – making it considerably slower than all Italian front-line fighters. Even the planners of the raid – codenamed Operation *Judgement* – expected heavy losses of both planes and crew. Still, with well-trained airmen, if the attack was pressed home aggressively, these biplanes might just inflict sufficient damage on Italy's battleship fleet to level the scales in the naval war for control of the Mediterranean.

In fact the raid on Taranto was a resounding success. The Italian Navy – the Regia Marina – had gathered all six of its battleships in the port, as well as cruisers, destroyers and other smaller warships. The first wave of 12 Swordfish attacked soon after 11.00pm. Six aircraft armed with torpedoes attacked the battleships, while the rest dropped bombs on other targets. Two battleships were badly damaged, while others were lucky to survive unscathed. Ninety minutes later the second wave of nine Swordfish launched its attack, and another battleship was hit. So, in less than two hours, the Regia Marina had lost half of its battleship force, all for the loss of just two aircraft. Of these ships, two would eventually return to service, but a third

HMS *Illustrious* was the first fleet carrier of its class, and while it had a limited capacity of 36 aircraft, its armoured flight deck made it more resilient than contemporary American or Japanese carrier designs. It joined the Mediterranean Fleet in August 1940.

was damaged beyond repair. The raiders had struck a decisive blow – the equivalent of a large-scale naval victory if it had been fought using more conventional means.

As a result, the Royal Navy gained effective control of the Mediterranean. While the Axis powers reacted decisively by diverting large numbers of German aircraft to the theatre, the attack gave the British exactly what they needed – a respite in the naval campaign, which they used to strengthen the defences of Malta and to put pressure on Italian supply routes to North Africa. These, however, were mere strategic implications of the raid. Its real significance lay in what it promised. The Taranto attack was the first time carrier-borne aircraft had been used to attack a heavily defended naval base. The raid not only revolutionized naval warfare, it also changed the course of the war.

It marked the end for the battleship as the arbiter of victory at sea. From that point on, the future of naval warfare would centre around the aircraft carrier, and the fighting potential of carrier-borne aircraft. Significantly, this demonstration of naval airpower was not lost on the Japanese. Just over a year later, the Imperial Japanese Navy would demonstrate just how effective a carrier-borne air strike of this kind could be, when launched on a much larger scale, using modern aircraft. Effectively, Taranto served as the blueprint for the Japanese attack on Pearl Harbor. Thanks to those 42 young airmen, naval warfare would never be the same again.

The Italian battleship *Conti di Cavour*, pictured on the morning of 12 November 1940. Its decks are awash, and it is sitting on the bottom of Taranto harbour, after being hit by a single torpedo the previous evening. It remained out of action for the remainder of the war.

CHRONOLOGY

1940

10 June	Italy declares war on Britain and France.
20 June	Start of the Battle of Britain.
22 June	French sign armistice.
28 June	Battle of the *Espero* Convoy – first significant but indecisive naval clash in Mediterranean.
3 July	Operation *Catapult* – destruction of French fleet at Oran and Mers-el-Kébir.
9 July	Indecisive battle of Calabria (also known as Punta Stilo). Italian battleship *Giulio Cesare* damaged.
19 July	Battle of Cape Spada – minor British victory – Italian light cruiser sunk.
23 August	Swordfish from *Eagle* bomb Italian ships off Bomba, Libya.
30 August	Operation *Hats* begins – reinforcements for Mediterranean Fleet leave Gibraltar.
26 September	Heavy Luftwaffe raids on London.
28 September	Signing of Tripartite Pact between Germany, Italy and Japan.
12 October	Battle of Cape Passero – minor British victory – three Italian light warships sunk.
28 October	Italian Army invades Greece.
4 November	Operation *MB8* begins.
5 November	Convoys MW3 and AN6 sail from Alexandria, bound for Crete and Greece.
6 November	Force A (including *Illustrious*) sails from Alexandria.
7 November	Force F and Force H sail from Gibraltar (Operation *Coat*).
	Convoy MW3 and Force B reach Suda Bay, Convoy AN6 detached to sail on to Piraeus.
	Forces B and C combine off Crete to form Force X. MW3 proceeds towards Malta.

8 November	Force A reaches a point 200 miles east of Malta, screening Convoy MW3.
	Force H detached from Force F, to carry out Operation *Crack*.
	Force X joins Force A.
9 November	Operation *Crack* – Swordfish from *Ark Royal* attack Italian airbase at Cagliari.
	Force H rejoins Force F – air attack on combined force by Italian bombers.
	Italians detect Force A – unsuccessful submarine attack on *Ramillies*.
10 November	Force A and Force F rendezvous off Pantelleria.
11 November	Force F puts in to Malta, to unload troops.
	Ramillies also enters Valetta to join Convoy ME3.
	Convoy MW3 reaches Malta; Convoy ME3 departs, bound for Alexandria.
	Noon: Force X detached from Force A to carry out attack on Strait of Otranto.
	6.00pm: *Illustrious* and escorts detached to carry out Operation *Judgement*.

Operation *Judgement* (11–12 November)

11 November

8.00pm:	*Illustrious* reaches Point X.
8.00–8.45pm:	Air raid in Taranto.
8.30pm:	First wave takes off.
9.15pm:	After sailing in a circle, *Illustrious* returns to Point X.
9.20pm:	Second wave takes off (two planes damaged).
9.44pm:	Swordfish L4Q takes off, and follows rest of flight.
9.45pm:	Hale given order to proceed.
10.00pm:	Aircraft partially dispersed amid thick clouds.

10.05pm:	L5Q loses fuel tank, and returns to carrier.
10.50pm:	Williamson sights Taranto.
10.56pm:	Williamson orders sub-flights to begin their approach.
11.10pm:	First wave's flares dropped to east of Mar Grande.
	Hale sights Taranto 60 miles ahead, due to glow from AA fire.
11.12pm:	Torpedo attacks by first wave begin.
11.35pm:	Attack by first wave ends.
11.55pm:	Hale orders sub-flights to begin their approach.

12 November

12.10am:	Second wave's flares dropped to east of Mar Grande.
12.11am:	Torpedo attacks by second wave begin.
12.35am:	Attack by second wave ends – completion of raid.
2.50am:	Last surviving aircraft returns to *Illustrious*.
1.20am:	Battle of the Strait of Otranto – British victory – small Italian convoy destroyed.
7.00am:	*Illustrious* rejoins the Mediterranean Fleet.

14 November	*Illustrious* returns to Alexandria, together with remainder of Home Fleet.
27 November	Battle of Cape Spartivento – inconclusive naval clash.

ORIGINS OF THE CAMPAIGN

In late 1940, naval aviation in the Royal Navy was largely seen as something of a gimmick, an untested and expensive diversion of resources from the main battle fleet. Naval battles were won by guns, not aircraft, and the job of aviators was to locate the enemy, spot the fall of shot in a gunnery duel, and – if all went well – use their bombs and torpedoes to harry the enemy as they withdrew. It was not until the potential of naval air strikes was demonstrated at Taranto that most senior Royal Navy commanders realized that aircraft and aircraft carriers offered them a new way of achieving victory at sea. Fortunately for the Fleet Air Arm, the commander who counted – Admiral Cunningham – was already convinced that naval aviation had a key role to play in his campaign against the Italian fleet.

Cunningham realized that airpower was the key to the war in the Mediterranean. By the autumn of 1939, the Italian Air Force had as many as 3,700 aircraft at its disposal, including 1,213 fighters and 1,510 bombers.

When used as a torpedo bomber, the Fairey Swordfish carried a single 18in. Mark XII torpedo, slung beneath its fuselage. It had a range of 1,500 yards at 40 knots, and carried a 388lb warhead.

Central Mediterranean, 1940

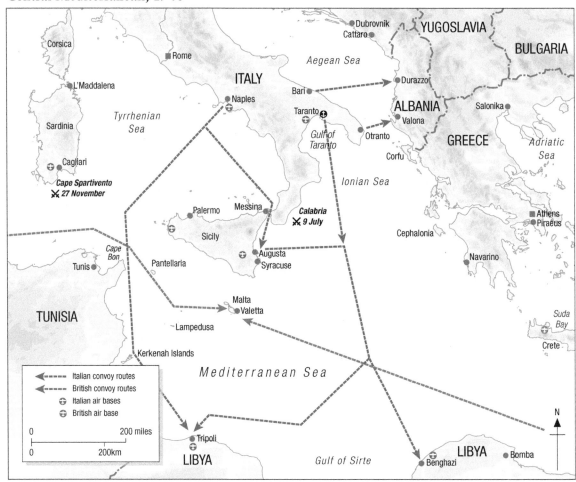

These totals included 417 virtually obsolete Fiat CR.32 biplane fighters, although they were in the process of being replaced by more modern aircraft, such as the Fiat G.50 'Freccia'. Of the Italian bomber fleet, the most numerous was the Savoia-Marchetti SM.79 'Sparviero', of which 413 were in service. By contrast the British had only 171 aircraft in the Mediterranean, stationed from Gibraltar to Palestine, of which 75 were fighters and the rest bombers. These numbers though, were bolstered by aircraft of the French Air Force – 152 fighters and 191 bombers – stationed in southern France, Corsica and French North Africa. Unfortunately for Cunningham, though, these aircraft would play no effective part in the campaign.

On 10 June, exactly a month after German troops crossed the French frontier, Mussolini's Italy declared war on both Britain and France. A week later, after German troops had occupied Paris, the French opened peace negotiations with Italy. On 22 June 1940, Marshal Pétain signed an armistice with Nazi Germany, and three days later a similar armistice was signed between France and Italy. This meant that, although the war in the Mediterranean was barely two weeks old, Britain found itself alone. At the time, the last British troops had just been evacuated from France, and the German Army was poised to launch an invasion across the English Channel.

All British resources – ships, men and aircraft – were needed to defend against a potential invasion of Britain. Therefore, Cunningham would have to fight his campaign with the limited resources he had available.

Many of the Royal Air Force (RAF) squadrons in the Mediterranean were deployed in defence of Egypt, where an Italian army was massed along the frontier. This left only a very few aircraft to defend Malta, which Cunningham regarded as the key to the Mediterranean – a vital staging post between Alexandria and Gibraltar. That meant that the single aircraft carrier in the theatre, and the limited number of aircraft carried on board, represented a priceless asset. It alone had the ability to strike the Italian fleet, either at sea or in harbour. This, though, was not a task the Fleet Air Arm was normally expected to carry out. The Admiralty had a very limited view of what naval aircraft could achieve, and so the roles the Fleet Air Arm was assigned before 1940 were restricted to reconnaissance and artillery spotting. This in turn was due to a lack of understanding of the full potential of naval aviation, which stemmed from the absence of a dedicated naval air wing during the inter-war period.

The Royal Naval Air Service (RNAS) was formed in July 1914, and by the end of World War I it had grown to a force of 2,500 aircraft and 55,000 personnel. During these years the navy made great strides in naval aviation, as first seaplane tenders were commissioned, and then a rudimentary aircraft carrier, HMS *Furious*. In August 1917 the first carrier landing was made on *Furious*, even though a second attempt led to the loss of the pilot. Lessons were learned, the flight deck was modified, and 'landing on' became much safer. In July 1918 aircraft from *Furious* launched a successful attack on the

The launch of the dreadnought *Giulio Cesare* in Genoa in June 1910. It was the first dreadnought to enter service with the Italian Navy, at which time it carried 13 30.5cm guns. During the 1930s its midships turret was removed, and it was rebuilt according to more modern lines.

German zeppelin base in Tondern (now Tønder in Denmark). This demonstrated that the Naval Air Service had potential as an offensive force. However, by then it no longer existed. In April 1918 the RNAS was merged with the Royal Flying Corps (RFC), to form the Royal Air Force (RAF). With a stroke of the pen the Royal Navy lost control of naval aviation, and by the end of the war its aircraft and airmen were transferred into this new service.

This meant that, during the 1920s, while the Royal Navy possessed its own aircraft carriers, it had to rely on the RAF to operate aircraft from them. This coincided with a dramatic reduction in the size of the RAF, and a consequent lack of suitable airmen experienced in carrier operations. In 1923 a dedicated Fleet Air Arm (FAA) branch of the RAF was formed, and gradually the situation began to improve. These FAA aircrews practised carrier operations using the two existing British aircraft carriers, *Furious* and *Argus*, which by 1930 had been joined by four more – *Glorious*, *Courageous*, and the smaller carriers *Eagle* and *Hermes*. The introduction of steam catapults and arrester gear made the launch and recovery of aircraft more efficient, and allowed larger numbers of aircraft to be embarked. By 1930 the Fleet Air Arm consisted of just over 300 aircraft – a respectable total, even though they were still part of the RAF.

By 1938 *Ark Royal* had joined the fleet, and a new breed of armoured carrier was under construction. The namesake of this new class would be HMS *Illustrious*, the aircraft of which would carry out the attack on Taranto.

In late 1940 the fighting core of the British Mediterranean Fleet comprised the aircraft carrier *Illustrious*, and a few battleships which first saw service in World War I. Here, *Illustrious* is accompanied by Cunningham's flagship *Warspite* (foreground), and the battleships *Resolution* and *Royal Sovereign*.

By then the political climate had changed. Another European war was looming, and the parsimony of the inter-war years came to an end; money was found for new ships, aircraft and servicemen. These Illustrious-class carriers were originally designed as replacements for the first generation of British aircraft carriers – *Furious*, *Argus*, *Hermes* and *Eagle* – but the growing threat of war meant that now even these old carriers would have to remain in service. This expansion prompted a new battle for the control of naval aviation. The Admiralty argued that a modern fleet needed its own organic air arm, and the government heeded its call.

Although the Admiralty gained formal control of the Fleet Air Arm only on 24 May 1939, the political decision had been made almost two years earlier, in July 1937. In between, the Royal Navy embarked on a dramatic fourfold expansion of the Fleet Air Arm, and even welcomed 1,500 RAF volunteers, who elected to transfer from one service to the other. Two decades of RAF neglect and government parsimony meant that the aircraft issued to the Fleet Air Arm compared unfavourably with those in other navies. The principal fighter was the Sea Gladiator – a biplane which was already seen as obsolete when it entered service in 1937. It was followed by two underwhelming two-seater monoplane fighter designs – the Blackburn Roc and the Fairey Fulmar, which entered service in 1939 and 1940 respectively. Neither aircraft was particularly effective, but while the Roc was quietly dropped from front-line service, the Fulmar remained the Fleet Air Arm's primary fighter until 1942.

In July 1936 the Fairey Swordfish became the Fleet Air Arm's multi-purpose reconnaissance aircraft, torpedo plane and bomber, although it also doubled as a naval gunnery spotter. This biplane was a flying museum piece compared with the latest American or Japanese monoplane bombers and torpedo planes, but British aircrews liked the robustness of the 'Stringbag', and it remained in service throughout the war, outliving the aircraft brought in to replace it. While the Swordfish was a good torpedo plane, its design made it unsuitable for use as a dive-bomber. Instead, a derivative of the Roc, the Blackburn Skua, combined the roles of dive-bomber and fighter. First introduced in 1938, the Skua remained in front-line service until 1941. In the Mediterranean it was deployed on board HMS *Ark Royal*. So, while the Fleet Air Arm entered the war against Italy with a selection of largely underpowered low-performance aircraft, the aircrews would simply have to make the most of them, until more modern replacements entered service.

The Italian Cavour-class battleships *Conti di Cavour* and *Giulio Cesare*, pictured during a goodwill visit to Malta in 1938. It was during this visit that Admiral Cunningham was able to tour the battleships, and met Ammiraglio di Squadra Riccardi, the Port Admiral in charge of Taranto in November 1940.

When Italy declared war on Britain on 10 June 1940, the only British aircraft carrier in the Mediterranean was HMS *Eagle*, which carried 18 Swordfish and three Sea Gladiators. This was barely enough to fulfil reconnaissance duties for the Mediterranean Fleet, let alone to provide a powerful enough air group to launch a major strike against the Italian battle fleet. Admiral Cunningham actually had a plan in place for this – an air strike against Italy's naval base at Taranto – but without more aircraft this scheme was impractical. The

Ammiraglio di Squadra Campioni's flagship *Conte di Cavour*, photographed from the bridge of its sister ship *Giulio Cesare* during the battle of Calabria (or Punta Stilo), fought on 9 July 1940. Campioni broke off the action after the *Giulio Cesare* was hit by a 15in. shell fired by *Warspite*.

capitulation of France tipped the strategic balance in the Mediterranean in favour of the Italians, but Cunningham retained the initiative by sending his ships into the central Mediterranean, and daring the Italians to give battle. The first major clash took place on 9 July, a month after the start of the campaign. This engagement, the battle of Calabria (or Punta Stilo) was inconclusive, but it was the Italians who withdrew, after the battleship *Giulio Cesare* was hit by a 15-inch shell fired from the British battleship *Warspite*. During the battle Swordfish from *Eagle* launched several small attacks against a force of Italian heavy cruisers, but all the torpedoes missed their targets.

This battle was fought because the Italian fleet put to sea to cover a troop convoy, sailing from Naples to Benghazi in North Africa. The British were in the area to protect their own convoys, sailing between Alexandria and Malta. On this occasion all the convoys reached port without incident, but the operation clearly demonstrated the naval dynamics at play in the central

The city of Taranto straddles two anchorages – the larger Mar Grande on its seaward side, and the Mar Piccolo to the north of the port. The two are connected by the Canale Navigabile, which also divides the city into two parts. In November 1940, smaller Italian warships and some cruisers were moored along or just off the naval quay running along the shore of the Mar Piccolo, on the northern side of the eastern portion of the city.

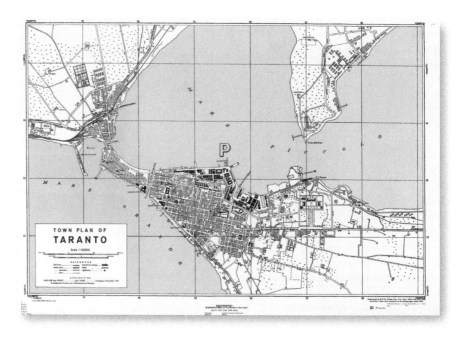

TOWN PLAN OF
TARANTO

Battle of Calabria (Punta Stilo), 9 July 1940, 3.45–4.15pm

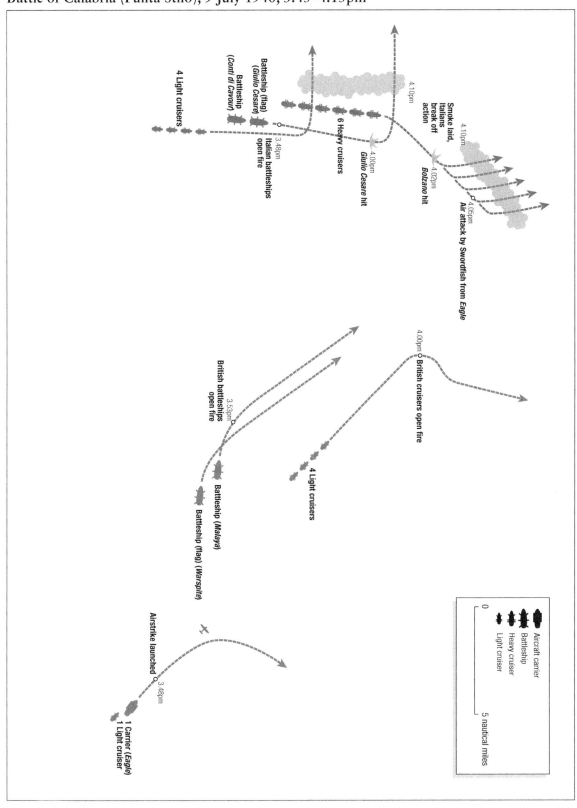

4 Light cruisers

Battleship
(*Conti di Cavour*)

Battleship (flag)
(*Giulio Cesare*)

3.48pm

4.00pm
Italian battleships
open fire

6 Heavy cruisers

4.00pm
Giulio Cesare hit

4.10pm

Smoke laid,
Italians
break off
action

4.02pm
Bolzano hit

4.05pm

4.10pm

4.00pm
Air attack by Swordfish from *Eagle*

British battleships
open fire

3.53pm

4.00pm British cruisers open fire

4 Light cruisers

Battleship (*Malaya*)

Battleship (flag) (*Warspite*)

Airstrike launched

3.48pm

1 Carrier (*Eagle*)
1 Light cruiser

Light cruiser
Heavy cruiser
Battleship
Aircraft carrier

0   5 nautical miles

17

Mediterranean. The British had to run convoys the length of the Mediterranean, from Egypt to Malta, and from Malta to Gibraltar. To the west of Malta convoys had to pass within range of Italian airbases in Sicily, while to the west the airbases were located in the south of the Italian peninsula. Just as importantly, convoys operating to the west of Malta passed relatively close to the Italian naval base at Taranto, forcing Cunningham to deploy the bulk of his battle fleet to support his convoys, in case the Italian fleet launched a sortie.

Similarly, this east–west convoy route bisected the Italian supply route between Italy and Libya, where their army was poised to invade British-held Egypt. This meant that the Italians had to provide heavy air and naval escorts for their own convoys. The waters to the south of Taranto and the west of Malta formed a strategic crossroads, where naval clashes were likely, and where the presence of the Italian battle fleet forced Cunningham to use his own battle fleet to support the movement of convoys through these dangerous waters. Malta itself was a useful base for the British, but it lacked adequate air defences, and was subject to repeated bombing by the Italian Air Force. However, it remained a thorn in the Italian side, as reconnaissance aircraft operating from the island were able to monitor the movements of the Italian battle fleet. This gave Cunningham a slight advantage in terms of intelligence gathering. It would also prove of inestimable value when he was given the chance to carry out his long-planned air attack on Taranto.

This opportunity presented itself in late August 1940. Reinforcements sent out from Britain finally arrived in Gibraltar, and after a brief stop they continued into the Mediterranean. The battleship *Valiant* and two light anti-aircraft cruisers were useful to Cunningham, but of greater importance was the brand-new aircraft carrier *Illustrious*. It had been commissioned on 26 May, and after embarking its squadrons it was sent to the West Indies for a 'work up' to assess the fighting potential of both ship and crew. On its return to Britain in late July it underwent a quick refit, and then set sail for the Mediterranean. During its journey eastward it was escorted by Force F, based in Gibraltar, and on 2 September it joined the Mediterranean Fleet off Pantelleria, an Italian-held island lying between Sicily and Tunisia. This meant that Cunningham now had the aircraft he needed to launch a carrier strike against Taranto. All he needed now was a suitable opportunity.

During the battle of Calabria (or Punta Stilo) an Italian heavy cruiser exchanges fire with British warships, to cover the withdrawal of Ammiraglio di Squadra Campioni's two battleships. Although the engagement was indecisive, it demonstrated that the Italian commander was overly cautious, largely because of the constraints imposed on him by his superiors.

OPPOSING COMMANDERS

ROYAL NAVY

In June 1939, **Admiral Sir Andrew Browne Cunningham** (1883–1963) became the new Commander-in-Chief of the British Mediterranean Fleet, hoisting his flag in the battleship HMS *Warspite*. This Dublin-born officer commanded a destroyer during World War I, and was awarded the Distinguished Service Order (DSO) during the conflict. He reached flag rank in 1932, and served as Rear Admiral, Destroyers, in the Mediterranean Fleet. Although other key appointments followed, his time in the Mediterranean gave him a clear understanding of the region. He was promoted to vice-admiral in 1936 and, in 1939, with the acting rank of admiral (confirmed in 1941), he was sent back to the Mediterranean, a command he described as 'The finest command the Royal Navy has to offer.'

Although the idea of an attack on Taranto had been developed by his predecessor, Admiral Sir Dudley Pound, Cunningham saw the merit of the operation, and supported Rear Admiral Lyster's plan to use carrier-based aircraft. Although he had little experience of carrier operations, he realized

As commander of the British Mediterranean Fleet in 1940, Admiral Sir Andrew B. Cunningham (1883–1963) realized that a carrier-borne attack on the Italian battleship fleet might help even the odds in the naval campaign he was waging for control of the Mediterranean.

both the value of intrinsic air support for his fleet, and the offensive potential of carrier strike aircraft. After Taranto, Cunningham went on to win a clear-cut victory over the Italian fleet at the battle of Matapan (1941), and then supervised the naval evacuation of Allied troops from Greece and Crete, despite heavy losses in ships and men. Cunningham then commanded the Allied naval effort during the landings in North Africa, Sicily and Italy, and oversaw the surrender of the Italian fleet in September 1943. The following month he returned to Britain to become First Sea Lord, and retired after the war with the rank of admiral of the fleet. He was deeply respected by his men, who popularly referred to him by his initials, 'ABC'. Today Cunningham is arguably regarded as the finest naval commander of the war.

Rear Admiral Lumley Lyster (1888–1957) joined the Royal Navy at the age of 14, and specialized in naval gunnery. He was awarded the DSO in 1917 while serving on board the cruiser *Cassandra*, and ended the war as a lieutenant commander. He was promoted to captain in 1928, and was given his first command – the cruiser *Danae* – in 1932. Between 1937 and 1939 Lyster commanded the aircraft carrier *Glorious*, while it was serving in the Mediterranean Fleet. It was during this period that he first developed plans for an air attack on the Italian battle fleet as it lay in port. He reached flag rank shortly before the outbreak of war, and was initially sent to Scapa Flow, where he served as Rear Admiral, Scapa. However, in August 1940 he was named the Mediterranean Fleet's Rear Admiral, Aircraft Carriers. Lyster raised his flag in the Royal Navy's latest aircraft carrier *Illustrious*, and on joining Cunningham's fleet he resurrected his plan for a carrier-borne air strike on the Italian fleet. He therefore supervised both the planning and execution of Operation *Judgement* – the Taranto raid. Lyster was a formidable but highly respected officer, who was a staunch advocate of the importance of naval aviation. He went on to command air operations in the Home Fleet, and during the Malta Convoy battles of 1942. Lyster retired in 1945, with the rank of vice-admiral.

Rear Admiral Lumley Lyster (1888–1957) was a passionate supporter of naval aviation, and he saw the Taranto raid as an opportunity to demonstrate its effectiveness. Pictured with him is Commander James I. Robertson (1902–76), who was in charge of flying operations on board *Illustrious*.

Rear Admiral Henry Pridham-Wippell (1885–1952) was another experienced officer who made his mark in small ships during World War I, commanding Britain's destroyers off Gallipoli and in the Adriatic. During the inter-war years Pridham-Wippell commanded a cruiser, but by 1932 he had returned to light forces, commanding destroyer flotillas in the Home Fleet. He reached flag rank in 1938, but when the war began he was serving ashore, in an administrative post at the Admiralty. It was not until November 1940 that he returned to sea, as second-in-command of the Mediterranean Fleet, and commander of its light forces. He flew his flag in the light cruiser *Orion*. During Operation *MB8*, Pridham-Wippell led the sweep of the Straits of Otranto that took place on the same night as the Taranto raid. He was promoted to vice-admiral, and was later knighted for the key part he played in the battle of Matapan (1941). He went on to command the Mediterranean Fleet's 1st Battle Squadron, until his flagship *Barham* was torpedoed. On returning to Britain he was given command of the Dover Patrol as Flag Officer, Dover, a post he held until the end of the war. He retired in 1948. Because of his unusual name, Pridham-Wippell was irreverently known as 'Pig and Whistle' by his men.

The aircrew members who took part in the attack on Taranto formed part of the crew of the aircraft carrier *Illustrious*, commanded by **Captain Denis Boyd** (1891–1965), who served as a torpedo officer during World War I, and who remained a torpedo expert until his appointment as commander of *Illustrious* in January 1940. He ended the war as a vice-admiral and Fifth Sea Lord. Flight operations on board *Illustrious* were supervised by **Commander (Flying) James I. Robertson** (1902–76), who first qualified as a pilot in 1926, and held both RN and RAF ranks until the navy officially gained control of the Fleet Air Arm in 1939. He was appointed to *Illustrious* while it was being fitted out, and remained with it until early 1941, when he was given command of the escort carrier *Archer*.

The two Fleet Air Arm officers destined to lead the two attack waves against Taranto were **Lieutenant Commander Kenneth Williamson** (1906–90) and **Lieutenant Commander J. W. Hale** (1902–69). 'Hooch' Williamson was the commanding officer of 815 Squadron, a post he had held since late July 1940, and was both a highly experienced pilot and a well-liked officer, whose natural air of calm and imperturbability was legendary. He joined the service in 1924, and qualified as a pilot five years later. Before joining *Illustrious*, he had been the commander of 822 Squadron. He was the ideal man to lead the first attack on Taranto. The second wave was led by 'Ginger' Hale, the commanding officer of 819 Squadron, a post held since February. With over two decades of service behind him, Hale was described as being 'as unshakable as the Rock of Gibraltar'. Before the war he had commanded squadrons in both *Courageous* and *Glorious*, and had served during the latter carrier's pre-war deployment in the Mediterranean, under Lyster. Hale was also a keen rugby player, and had played both for the Navy and for England.

Lieutenant Commander Kenneth Williamson (1906–90) was the commanding officer of 815 Squadron, Fleet Air Arm, and led the first wave of aircraft during the Taranto raid. He was shot down during the operation, and spent the remainder of the war in prison camps in Italy and Germany.

REGIA MARINA

Cunningham's counterpart in the Regia Marina (Italian Royal Navy) was **Ammiraglio di Squadra Inigo Campioni** (1878–1944). Born in Tuscany, Campioni joined the navy when he was 15, and served on a variety of ships, including the cruiser *Amalfi* during the brief Italo-Turkish War (1912–13), and the battleship *Conte di Cavour* during World War I. In 1916 he was given command of the destroyer *Ardito*, and in late 1917 he distinguished himself during an engagement with Austro-Hungarian forces in the Adriatic. He was duly awarded the Bronze Medal of Military Valour for his actions. Campioni remained in the navy after the war, and promotion was followed by a key land-based appointment, as the head of a weapons development programme based in La Spezia. In 1929 he was given command of the battleship *Caio Duilio*. Five years later he was promoted to *ammiraglio di divisione* (rear admiral), and commanded a cruiser force during the Italian invasion of Abyssinia (1935–36).

In 1936, Campioni was promoted to *ammiraglio di squadra* (vice-admiral), prior to becoming the navy's Deputy Chief of Staff. In this capacity he developed plans for a naval conflict with both Britain and France. He returned to sea in 1939 as commander of the 1st Battle Squadron – the Italian battleship force – and flew his flag in the *Giulio Cesare*. Effectively this made him the commander of the main Italian battle fleet. When Italy entered the war Campioni's main priority was the safe transit of convoys to North Africa – a task he performed with great skill. However, in July 1940 his fleet encountered part of Cunningham's Mediterranean Fleet off Calabria, and withdrew after one of his battleships received minor damage. This was due less to a lack of aggression on Campioni's part than to the constraints imposed upon him by the naval high command. At Taranto his fleet was well protected, and it is unfair to criticize Campioni too harshly for the losses it suffered during the raid.

Campioni retained his command, but after the battle of Cape Spartivento fought two weeks later, he was accused of undue caution, and was relieved of his command in early December 1940. He went on to become Governor of the Italian Dodecanese – its islands in the Aegean – a post he held until Italy's surrender in September 1943. His refusal to capitulate to the Germans led to his arrest and imprisonment by Mussolini's rump government, based in northern Italy. His continued loyalty to the kingdom of Italy rather than Mussolini's Social Republic led to his trial, conviction and execution in May 1944. Despite his lack of success against the Royal Navy, Campioni was probably the most competent admiral in the Regia Marina during the war. He might have achieved more had he not been constantly dogged by supply problems, restrictive orders and political interference.

Ammiraglio di Squadra Inigo Campioni (1878–1944) was the commander of the Italian battle fleet in 1940, and led it into action at the battle of Calabria. He was deemed responsible for the fleet's failures during the opening months of the war, and was relieved of his command four weeks after the attack on Taranto.

While Campioni commanded the battle fleet, **Ammiraglio di Squadra Arturo Riccardi** (1878–1966) was the man in charge of the defence of Taranto. Riccardi hailed from Pavia, and initially pursued a military rather than a naval career. He first saw action in China with the Fanteria Real Marina (Royal Marine Infantry, or marines) during the Boxer Rebellion (1899–1901). He remained with what became the Brigata Marina (Marine Brigade) during World War I, and saw further action against the Austro-Hungarians. He also served at sea, and ended the war as a highly decorated and well-respected officer, with experience on both land and sea. After the war Riccardi held a variety of shore-based appointments, and in 1925 he joined the National Fascist Party, despite his deeply held religious beliefs. This boosted his career, and in 1932 he reached flag rank. He became an *ammiraglio di squadra* in 1935. A naval command followed, and an appointment to the Italian Senate. In 1938 his squadron paid an official visit to Malta, and he entertained Cunningham on board his flagship. During the visit, Riccardi revealed that he kept a biography of Nelson beside his bed. Cunningham later commented that he seemed not to have benefited from it. In December 1940, Riccardi was the rear admiral in charge of Taranto naval base, a post he had held for almost a year. His defences were adequate, but production delays, mishaps and arguably a lack of drive on Riccardi's part meant that what could have been a near-impregnable naval base was penetrated with relative ease by the Swordfish of the Fleet Air Arm. Immediately after Taranto, Riccardi became Chief of Staff of the navy, a post he held until Italy's surrender.

The man who replaced Campioni as commander of the Italian battle fleet was **Ammiraglio di Squadra Angelo Iachino** (1889–1976). The Ligurian joined the navy in 1904, and during World War I he commanded a torpedo boat. He distinguished himself, and promotion followed. During the 1920s Iachino served as Italy's naval attaché in China, and on his return to Italy in 1928 he was given command of a destroyer. Other commands followed – for instance, during 1936–37 Iachino commanded a light squadron, operating off the Spanish coast in support of General Franco's nationalist rebels. By 1939 his cruisers were in action again, this time supporting the Italian invasion of Albania. When the war began Iachino held the rank of *ammiraglio di squadra*, and commanded the cruiser forces of Campioni's battle fleet. He displayed both aggression and skill during the battle of Calabria, fought in July 1940, and unlike Campioni his performance was viewed favourably by his naval and political superiors. His cruisers were relatively unscathed during the Swordfish attack on Taranto. He succeeded Campioni as commander of the Italian battle fleet in December 1940, a post he held until February 1943, despite his defeats at Matapan and Sirte.

One of the advantages the British enjoyed in the Mediterranean was radar. *Illustrious* carried a Type 79 (Air Warning) set, and during Operation *MB8* no fewer than 15 British warships were equipped with similar radars, which provided early warning of enemy air attack, and allowed combat air patrol fighters to intercept enemy reconnaissance aircraft.

The Fairey Fulmar was a two-seater aircraft, which, while slower than its more modern Italian or German counterpart, was the best fighter available to the Fleet Air Arm in 1940. This aircraft was primarily used to screen carriers and convoys from enemy air attack.

Finally **Ammiraglio di Divisione Carlo Bergamini** (1888–1943), who commanded the battleship squadron which suffered directly during the Taranto raid, was generally regarded as a competent and conscientious naval officer. He was born near Modena, and joined the navy in 1904. He specialized in gunnery, and served in cruisers during the Italo-Turkish War and World War I. Shortly before the end of the war he was decorated for bravery, following a brush with Austro-Hungarian forces in the northern Adriatic. During the inter-war period he rose steadily through the ranks, and was given his first command – a destroyer – in 1925. He attained flag rank in 1933, and when Italy entered the war he was serving as Campioni's Chief of Staff. He saw action during the battle of Calabria, and was subsequently named the commander of the 9th Division – the fleet's Littorio-class battleships – flying his flag in the *Vittorio Veneto*. In 1943 he replaced Iachino as commander of the Italian battle fleet, and was killed when his flagship *Roma* was sunk by a German glide bomb as it and the rest of the fleet were steaming south to surrender to the Allies. Bergamini was buried at sea.

OPPOSING FORCES

ROYAL NAVY

The attack on Taranto on the evening of 11 November 1940 formed the climax of a much larger British naval operation. Codenamed *MB8*, this larger enterprise also involved the escort of reinforcements from Britain, the screening of three convoys, the transport of troops and equipment to Greece and Crete, and a sweep of the Straits of Otranto. This large and complex operation involved a large portion of Admiral Cunningham's Mediterranean Fleet, as well as Vice-Admiral Somerville's Force H, based in Gibraltar. The fighting heart of the Mediterranean Fleet was its battleship fleet, which consisted of three ageing Queen Elizabeth-class battleships, as well as one of the Royal Sovereign class. The reinforcements from Britain included another Queen Elizabeth-class – *Barham*. These battleships had all seen service during World War I – in fact most of them had fought at the battle of Jutland (1916).

Four Swordfish ranged around the forward lift of HMS *Illustrious*, during operations in early 1940, before the aircraft carrier was badly damaged during a mass air attack by Fliegerkorps X. The Swordfish still have their wings folded back – the way they were stored in the hangar.

While most of Britain's dreadnought fleet was scrapped after the war, these nine battleships in two classes were spared, as their armament of eight 15-inch guns apiece was considered too great an asset to lose. Therefore they formed the core of Britain's battle fleet during the inter-war years, during which they were augmented by two more British battleships of the Nelson class, each of which carried nine 16-inch guns. During this period the nine older battleships were all modified to varying degrees, and therefore they still remained useful members of the fleet in 1940. Most significantly their anti-aircraft armament had been improved during the inter-war years, as had their gun mountings and fire control systems. A by-product of this was that the range of their guns was increased. By 1940 they also carried radar, which gave them a distinct advantage over their Italian counterparts.

However, they were all slow, particularly when compared with Italian battleships of the Littorio class. This was particularly so for the Royal Sovereign-class battleships, which were no longer considered fast enough to operate in company with Cunningham's other battleships. During the battle of Calabria in July 1940, *Warspite* scored a hit on the Italian battleship *Giulio Cesare* at a range of 12 nautical miles, which prompted the Italian battle fleet to disengage. This demonstrated the effectiveness of these old battleships, and the accuracy of British gunnery direction. A screen of heavy cruisers, light cruisers and destroyers also formed part of Cunningham's force during Operation *MB8*, but for the most part their role was largely a supporting one. However, Pridham-Wippell's force of three light cruisers and two destroyers was given a more offensive role, conducting a sweep of the Straits of Otranto.

Cunningham's other main asset was the aircraft carrier *Illustrious*, the namesake of its class. It joined the Mediterranean Fleet in August 1940, and Cunningham put it to immediate use, attacking Italian airfields in the Aegean and North Africa. In theory, Cunningham also had the use of the smaller aircraft carrier *Eagle*, but in early November it was forced to undergo a refit in Alexandria, and so was unable to participate in Operation *MB8*. Both carriers carried Swordfish as strike aircraft, while *Illustrious* also carried a squadron of Fulmars, which provided it with fighter protection. *Illustrious* could carry 36 aircraft – three squadrons of 12 aircraft apiece. So, in November 1941, it carried 24 Swordfish from 815 and 819 Squadrons and 12 Fulmars from 806 Squadron. Because of losses and damage, five replacement Swordfish from *Eagle* (813 and 824 Squadrons) were transferred to *Illustrious* for the duration of the operation. A total of 21 Swordfish took part in the raid.

Officially designated the Fairey Swordfish TSR Mark I, this aircraft was designed to carry a crew of three – pilot, observer and gunner. However, for the attack on Taranto – Operation *Judgement* – long-range fuel tanks had

Captain Denis Boyd was the commanding officer of HMS *Illustrious*, and therefore the man responsible for making sure the orders of Rear Admiral Lyster were carried out. He was a popular captain, and was seen by many young Fleet Air Arm crew members as a father figure.

to be fitted, and the only place to house them was above the middle cockpit. This meant there was space for only one man in addition to the pilot – the observer. The hope was that as it was a nocturnal surprise attack, there would be no need to defend the aircraft from enemy fighters. In that eventuality the observer would just have to fight the enemy off as best he could. The Swordfish was primarily a torpedo plane, designed to carry a single Mark XII torpedo slung beneath its fuselage. Alternatively, up to three bombs could be carried under each wing. The 'Stringbag', as it was affectionately known by its crew, was not designed to act as a dive-bomber, so these bombs were dropped while making a level attack run. Similarly the torpedo had to be launched while flying at a relatively low height – approximately 80ft – and while heading directly towards the target if it was stationary, or slightly ahead of it if the ship was under way.

Above all the Swordfish was slow. While official tables give its maximum speed as 143mph when fully laden with a torpedo, Fleet Air Arm crews deny this, claiming that its top speed was never more than 100mph. It was also large, making it an easier target to hit. On a more positive note, the Swordfish was extremely manoeuvrable, and because of its construction it was also resistant to damage. Aircrews discovered that their Swordfish could be badly damaged, but would still be able to fly. Still, the 'Stringbag' was an ungainly aircraft and, in an age of fast monoplanes, it looked like a plane from an earlier era. Apparently, when a US naval aviator first saw the strange-looking biplane, he asked a British officer where the aircraft had come from. 'Fairey's' was the reply. 'That figures' responded the American.

Fairey Swordfish TSR, Mark I

Crew: three (pilot, observer and radio operator/rear gunner)

Length: 35ft 8in.

Wingspan: 45ft 6in.

Height: 12ft 4in.

Wing area: 607ft^2

Weight when laden: 7,580lb

Engine: Bristol Pegasus III radial engine

Maximum speed: 143mph when laden

Range: 522mi (455 nautical miles)

Endurance: 5½ hours

Ceiling: 16,500ft

Rate of Climb: 870ft/min at sea level, 690ft/min at 5,000ft

Armament:

Mark XII 18in. torpedo *or* 1,500 pounds of bombs carried under fuselage and wings

Note: Flares, rockets or even a 1,500lb mine could also be carried if required.

1 x forward-firing .303in. Vickers machine gun

1 x .303in. Lewis or Vickers K machine gun on swivel mount, in rear cockpit

Normally a Fairey Swordfish had a three-man crew – pilot, observer and telegraphist/air gunner. However, during the Taranto raid the presence of an external long-range fuel tank mounted over the observer's cockpit (or beneath it in bomb-armed planes) meant that the rear gunner was left behind.

ORDER OF BATTLE – OPERATION *MB8*

FORCE A
Warspite (Queen Elizabeth-class battleship) Flagship, Admiral Cunningham
Valiant (Queen Elizabeth-class battleship)
Malaya (Queen Elizabeth-class battleship)
Ramillies (Royal Sovereign-class battleship)
Illustrious (Illustrious-class aircraft carrier) Flagship, Rear Admiral Lyster

FORCE B
Sydney (Sydney-class light cruiser – Royal Australian Navy)
Ajax (Leander-class light cruiser)
Two destroyers

FORCE C
Orion (Leander-class light cruiser) Flagship, Rear Admiral Pridham-Wippell

FORCE F
Barham (Queen Elizabeth-class battleship)
Berwick (County-class heavy cruiser)
Glasgow (Town-class light cruiser)
Three destroyers

FORCE H
Ark Royal (Ark Royal-class aircraft carrier) Flagship, Vice-Admiral Somerville
Sheffield (Town-class light cruiser)
Eight destroyers

CONVOY MW-3
York (York-class heavy cruiser)
Gloucester (Town-class light cruiser)
Coventry (C-class light AA cruiser)
Three destroyers
Seven merchant ships

REGIA MARINA

Like Britain's Mediterranean Fleet, the fighting potential of the Italian Navy was centred around its battleships. At the start of 1940 this consisted of four warships – the two sister ships *Conte di Cavour* and *Giulio Cesare*, and another pair, the *Caio Diulio* and *Andrea Doria*. All four dated from World War I. The two Conti di Cavour-class ships were dreadnoughts, which joined the fleet in 1914–15, and carried 13 12in. guns in three triple and two twin turrets. During the inter-war period these dreadnoughts were extensively modernized, and their midships turret was removed, while their remaining barrels were re-bored as 32cm pieces. While these guns compared unfavourably with the eight 15in. mounted in their British counterparts, the larger salvo – ten shells rather than eight – meant that the weight of salvo was actually greater than those fired by British ships.

The two Caio Diulio-class battleships *Caio Diulio* and *Andrea Doria* entered service during 1915–16, and the two dreadnoughts carried a similar armament to the Conti di Cavour-class vessels. In fact the two classes were similar to the earlier ships, but incorporated a number of improvements in their configuration, light armament and gunnery fire control. During the 1930s they too were converted into modern battleships, armed in a similar manner to the pair of Conti di Cavour-class battleships. When Italy entered the war these battleships were earmarked to form the 1st (Battleship) Squadron of the Italian Fleet, and were based in Taranto. However, in

The modern Italian battleship *Littorio* was completed in May 1940, and joined the battle fleet at Taranto shortly afterwards. Its powerful armament of nine 38cm guns made it more than a match for the older British battleships of the Mediterranean Fleet.

June 1940 *Caio Diulio* was just completing a refit, and it rejoined the fleet on 15 July. By the time these two battleships had joined the squadron, the *Conti di Cavour* and the *Giulio Cesare* had already seen action in the battle of Calabria (9 July). Ammiraglio di Squadra Campioni broke off the action when *Giulio Cesare* was hit, but the damage was repaired by the end of August.

Like its sister ship, the *Andrea Doria* was also undergoing a major refit when Italy entered the war, and it joined the squadron only on 26 October. That was barely two weeks before the attack on Taranto, and it was still 'working up', and so officially was not an active part of the battleship squadron. However, two new additions to the Italian fleet arrived in Taranto in late May. These were the two brand-new Littorio-class battleships *Littorio* and *Vittorio Veneto*. Unlike their four predecessors these were modern battleships, built during the 1930s, and their design reflected this. They were faster than the squadron's older battleships, and carried a considerably more powerful armament of nine 38cm guns, mounted in three triple turrets. These two battleships were considered more than a match for the older British battleships of the Mediterranean Fleet, and their presence in the squadron gave Campioni a considerable degree of tactical and operational flexibility.

This battleship squadron was supported by other vessels, most notably the heavy cruisers under Ammiraglio di Squadra Iachino's command. These though, like the destroyer flotilla stationed in Taranto, were there to screen the battleships, and while they were capable of operating independently of the main battle fleet, Campioni preferred to keep them at hand, to counter the firepower of Cunningham's cruisers, or to provide a destroyer screen to protect the fleet's capital ships. What Campioni lacked was an aircraft carrier. The only air assets he had, apart from float planes carried on battleships and heavy cruisers, was the small seaplane carrier *Giuseppi Miraglia*, which carried 17 search aircraft. Mussolini regarded the whole of Italy as an aircraft carrier, poised to dominate the entire central Mediterranean. However, in June 1940 he approved the purchase of the passenger liner *Roma*, for conversion into the aircraft carrier *Aquila*. Work on it began only in late 1941, and it was not finished by the time Italy surrendered in September 1943.

This meant that if Campioni wanted air support, he had to request it from the Italian Air Force. While on paper this was a powerful force, for political, logistical and bureaucratic reasons these aircraft were not always available when the admiral requested them. Even then, the first months of the war demonstrated that Italian bombers such as the S-79 Sparviero, the SM-981 Pipistrello and the BR-20 Cicogna were not particularly good at attacking enemy warships. Numerous high-altitude attacks were made against Cunningham's ships, but very few hits were achieved. In 1939 the S-79 was reconfigured to carry torpedoes as well as bombs, but problems with release mechanisms and attack techniques meant that it was 1941 before these torpedo-armed bombers began to prove their worth.

So, while Cunningham's fleet ran the risk of suffering heavy air attacks when it entered the waters of the central Mediterranean, the risk to his ships was deemed to be relatively low. His main threat came from Campioni's capital ships, particularly now they had been reinforced by two modern and well-armed battleships. As long as the Italian battle fleet remained in Taranto, it posed an immense latent threat to the British. Every convoy passing within range of Taranto had to be escorted, and so major convoy movements – Cunningham's 'MB' operations – had to be covered by the outnumbered battleships of the Mediterranean Fleet. That was why Cunningham was keen to launch an air raid on the Italian port, however risky an enterprise it might be.

The *Vittorio Veneto* was the sister ship of the *Littorio*. Unlike the older battleships of the Italian fleet, the two ships benefited from the Pugliese system of underwater protection, where a hollow cylindrical drum supposedly protected the ships from torpedo attack.

Taranto

The port of Taranto was extremely well defended, as befitted the home base of the Italian battle fleet. The port consisted of an outer harbour (Mar Grande) and an inner harbour (Mar Piccolo), which were separated by a small canal, which ran between the two parts of the city. The heart of the navy base was traditionally the older portion that lay to the east of the canal, on the southern edge of the Mar Piccolo. Here a wharf and a string of jetties formed a sheltered anchorage for the lighter units of the fleet, including the odd cruiser. Warships up to the size of heavy cruisers could also lie at anchor in the Mar Piccolo itself. The main anchorage though, lay on the eastern side of the Mar Grande. It was here that the battleships were moored, sheltered behind a curved mole known as the Diga di Tarantola. A number of cruisers and destroyers also used the Mar Grande, although they tended to be moored on the outer fringes of the large anchorage. To the east of the anchorage an array of harbour facilities were located, including a large oil storage depot, a dry dock and a berth for a floating dock.

The Mar Grande was protected from the sea by a second mole, the Diga di San Vito, and a pair of submerged breakwaters, which ran in a curve around the anchorage, joining the small islands of Isoletto San Paolo and San Pietro to the Italian mainland. Gun batteries on the two islands and on the mainland offered protection against attack from enemy surface ships, although the likelihood of this sort of attack was considered low, as regular air patrols scoured the Gulf of Taranto, and an approaching enemy surface force would be detected before it reached the port. It could then be attacked by the Italian Air Force, and finished off by the battle fleet. So, the most significant threat to the base came from an attack launched by aircraft or submarines. It was hoped that an approaching enemy bomber force would be located by aerial reconnaissance, giving time for the air force to intercept the attackers. Failing that, a plan was in place for Italian fighters to fly combat air patrols over the harbour, where they could engage the bombers before they reached their targets.

In case enemy bombers were not detected by Italian air patrols, a string of 13 sound detection devices were placed around the harbour. They were designed to pick up the sound of aircraft from up to 25 nautical miles away from the port, providing enough time to sound the harbour's air raid warning sirens, and for all the gun crews in the port and in the fleet to man their guns. Although this gave insufficient time to provide a combat air patrol screen over the harbour, at least Italian fighters would arrive in time to harry the enemy bombers after they carried out their attack. The port's main anti-aircraft defences consisted of 21 batteries of 10.2cm (4in.) guns, 13 of which were mounted in shore batteries, and another eight on barges anchored around the periphery of the Mar Grande. These guns were also dual purpose, and so were capable of engaging enemy surface ships such as destroyers or torpedo boats, as well as aircraft. Unfortunately they were all guns of World War I vintage, and lacked the rate of fire needed to build up a truly effective flak barrage.

The fire of these anti-aircraft batteries was augmented by automatic cannon and machine-gun positions: 84 2cm Breda guns, and 109 13.2mm Breda machine guns, all in single or double anti-aircraft mountings. While these were effective weapons, they had a limited range, and so were constrained by their siting. To help these guns locate their targets, 22 searchlights were mounted around the harbour. In the event of an air attack

Taranto Harbour Defences, November 1940

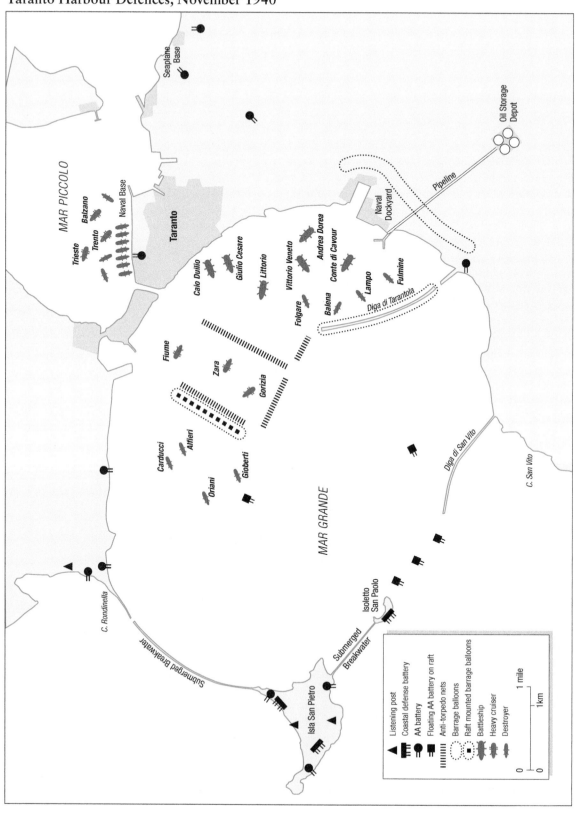

these guns and searchlights were, of course, augmented by the guns and searchlights of the warships anchored in the harbour. However, it appears that no clear fire plan had been created, and coordination between ship-based and land-based gun and searchlight crews was minimal.

A more passive form of defence was provided by a hydrophone station on the island of San Pietro, designed to listen for approaching enemy submarines, and a string of torpedo nets, sited to protect the most important elements of the battle fleet. It had been estimated that just over 13,800 yards of steel torpedo netting was required to protect the warships adequately in the anchorage, but only 4,550 yards of this was actually in place when the British launched their air attack on Taranto. A further 3,140 yards of it were still coiled up in a naval yard on the eastern side of the anchorage, waiting to be put in place. While this lack of anti-torpedo netting was largely due to supply problems, the delay in putting the remaining available netting in place was largely the fault of the fleet's commanders. The reason for this was a matter of compromise.

It took time to open and close the nets using tugs and support vessels, which in turn added to the time it took for the battle fleet to put to sea. Campioni had ordered four main lines of nets to be rigged, but there were gaps between them, allowing his warships to manoeuvre through the defences. So, three strings of anti-torpedo nets ran from the tip of the Diga di Tarantola towards the centre of the Mar Grande, and then northwards towards the mainland, just to the west of the western side of the city. A fourth net ran northwards from a point west of the breakwater towards the canal, dividing the protected anchorage in two. The battleships all lay to the east of this net. So, while these defences were adequate, and offered a practical solution to Campioni's problem of fleet manoeuvrability, the defences were incomplete. They could be penetrated by a daring submarine commander, or by pilots willing to run the gauntlet of the air defences, to attack the battleships moored in the eastern portion of the harbour.

Like its sister ship the *Andrea Doria*, the *Caio Duilio* was built as a dreadnought, and then modernized during the inter-war period. While its 30.5cm guns were smaller than those of its British counterparts, it carried ten of them, which gave it a broadly equivalent degree of firepower.

Finally a string of barrage balloons surrounded the battleship anchorage, running along the eastern shore of the Mar Grande, along the length of the Diga di Tarantola, and from a series of rafts moored along the line of the westernmost anti-torpedo net. Approximately 90 of these should have been in place, but shortages of hydrogen meant that not all of them were kept inflated all the time. Then, during the first week in November, a storm had damaged these defences, destroying balloons and severing tethering cables. As a result, only 27 barrage balloons were in place when the British launched their attack. For the Fleet Air Arm pilots, the long wingspan of the Swordfish – 45ft 6in. – meant that the torpedo planes had to pass beneath the level of the balloons, and at night it was impossible to see the cables, which were approximately 200 yards apart. Therefore avoiding them was entirely a matter of luck.

Conti di Cavour-class battleship

(Two in class) *Conti di Cavour, Giulio Cesare*

Laid down: 1910; Launched: 1911; Entered service: 1914–15

Displacement: 29,100 tons (29,600 tons fully laden)

Length: 186.4m; Beam: 33.1m

Draught: *Cavour*: 10m; *Cesare*: 10.42m

Armament: 10 x 32cm in two triple and two twin turrets

12 x 12cm guns in six twin turrets

eight x 10cm AA guns in four twin turrets

12 x 3.7cm AA guns, in six twin mounts

12 x 2cm AA guns, in six twin mounts

Armour: belt: 25cm, reducing to 8–13cm towards bow and stern; deck: 13.5–16.5cm; turrets and barbettes: 13–28cm

Propulsion: two turbines, eight boilers, producing 75,000shp; Maximum speed: 27 knots

Radius: 6,400 nautical miles at 13 knots

Crew: 1,236 men

Caio Duilio-class battleship

(Two in class) *Caio Duilio, Andrea Doria*

Laid down: 1912; Launched: 1913; Entered service: 1915–16

Displacement: *Duilio*: 26,434 tons (29,391 tons fully laden)

 Doria: 25,924 tons (28,882 tons fully laden)

Length: 186.9m; Beam: 28m

Draught: 9.4m

Armament: 10 x 32cm in two triple and two twin turrets

12 x 13.5cm guns in four triple turrets

10 x 9cm AA guns in 10 single turrets

15 x 3.7cm AA guns, in six twin and three single mounts

16 x 2cm AA guns, in eight twin mounts

Armour: belt: 25cm, reducing to 8–13cm towards bow and stern; deck: 9.8–12.5cm; turrets and barbettes: 13–28cm

Propulsion: two turbines, eight boilers, producing 75,000shp; Maximum Speed: 26 knots

Radius: 6,400 nautical miles at 13 knots

Crew: 1,485 men

Littorio-class battleship

(Two + two in class) *Littorio, Vittorio Veneto* (two more under construction in 1940)

Laid down: 1934; Launched: 1937; Entered service: 1940

Displacement: 40,516 tons (45,029 tons fully laden)

Length: 237.8m; Beam: 32.8m

Draught: 9.6m

Armament: 9 x 38cm in three triple turrets

12 x 15.2cm guns in four triple turrets

12 x 9cm AA guns in 12 single mounts

20 x 3.7cm AA guns, in eight twin and four single mounts

15 x 2cm AA guns, in eight twin mounts

Aircraft: One catapult, three x Ro.43 float planes

Armour: belt: 28cm, reducing to 13cm towards bow and stern; deck: 15–21cm; turrets and barbettes: 15–35cm

Propulsion: four turbines, eight boilers, producing 95,600shp; Maximum Speed: 26 knots

Radius: 4,580 nautical miles at 16 knots

Crew: 1,842 men

ORDER OF BATTLE – OPERATION *MB8*

1ST (BATTLESHIP) SQUADRON

5th Division

Conti di Cavour (Conti di Cavour-class battleship)

Giulio Cesare (Conti di Cavour-class battleship)

Andrea Doria (Caio Diulio-class battleship)

9th Division

Littorio (Littorio-class battleship)

Vittorio Veneto (Littorio-class battleship)

Caio Duilio (Caio Diulio-class battleship)

2ND (CRUISER) SQUADRON

1st Division

Pola (Zara-class heavy cruiser)

Zara (Zara-class heavy cruiser)

Goriza (Zara-class heavy cruiser)

Fiume (Zara-class heavy cruiser)

3rd Division

Trento (Trento-class heavy cruiser)

Trieste (Trento-class heavy cruiser)

Bolzano (Trento-class heavy cruiser)

8th Division

Duca degli Abruzzi (Duca degli Abruzzi-class light cruiser)

Giuseppe Garibaldi (Duca degli Abruzzi-class light cruiser)

Attached: *Giuseppe Miraglia* (Miraglia-class seaplane carrier)

4TH DESTROYER FLOTILLA

Alfredo Oriani, Giosui Carducci, Vincenzo Gioberti, Vittorio Alfieri (Oriani class)

Libeccio (Maestrale class)

Baleno, Lampo, Folgore (Folgore class)

PLANNING

The initial plan for a carrier-launched attack on Taranto was first conceived in 1935. As a result of Italy's invasion of Abyssinia, Admiral Fisher, commanding the British Mediterranean Fleet, felt that Britain and Italy might find themselves at war with each other. He therefore asked for plans to be drawn up for a carrier-borne attack on the Italian anchorage, using aircraft flying from HMS *Glorious*. However, the British government did little to intervene, and the scheme was quietly shelved. Three years later, Nazi Germany annexed Austria, prompting a major international crisis. This raised the prospect of war between Britain and Germany. The ideological links between Germany and Italy, and the growing friendship between Hitler and Mussolini meant that, in the event of a war in Europe, it was likely that the two fascist countries would form an alliance. Admiral Fisher's replacement, Admiral Pound, deemed it prudent to resurrect the plan, and so he summoned Captain Lyster of the *Glorious* to his flagship, the battleship *Queen Elizabeth*.

Admiral Dudley Pound (1877–1943) commanded the British Mediterranean Fleet until the summer of 1939, when he became First Sea Lord. It was Pound who authorized the planning of a carrier-borne strike against Taranto, even though he remained unconvinced of the effectiveness of such an operation.

A PLAN OF ATTACK

Only weeks before, the growing international tension had led to Pound's moving the Mediterranean Fleet from Malta to the less exposed naval base at Alexandria. It was there that Lyster was ordered to draw up a plan for an attack on the Italian battle fleet at Taranto – a pre-emptive strike, designed to cripple Italy's ability to fight a naval campaign in the Mediterranean. Pound did not expect that *Glorious* and its aircraft would survive the attack, as he knew that the Italians could marshal overwhelming numbers of aircraft against the British force. When Lyster returned to *Glorious* he began working on the plan, with the assistance of Commander Guy Willoughby (Commander, Flying) and Commander Lachlan Mackintosh (Senior Observer). The three men pulled out the old plan of 1935, and began adapting it to suit Admiral Pound's requirements.

It was clear that any attack had to be made at night, to improve the chances of surprise, and to reduce casualties. Fortunately *Glorious*' aircrews had been practising night flying for some time, and the

prospect of attacking under the cover of darkness held no great problems for them. Still, Lyster initiated an intense period of night flying and dummy attack training, using the battleships of the Mediterranean Fleet as targets. While Swordfish carrying torpedoes would be used to attack the Italian battleships berthed in the Mar Grande, a diversionary attack by Swordfish carrying bombs would be made on shore installations and suitable targets in the Mar Piccolo. To illuminate the area, other Swordfish would drop flares around the perimeter of the anchorage, and then join in the attack by bombing targets of opportunity. Willoughby estimated that the attackers would suffer around ten per cent casualties. This daring plan was eventually approved by Admiral Pound. However, it remained a contingency – one that the fleet commander did not share, even with his superiors at the Admiralty.

Eventually though, the crisis passed, and the plan was shelved. It has been claimed that Pound had little faith in carrier-borne air attacks, and would have preferred to launch his pre-emptive attack from Malta, before the island's airfields were put out of action by Italian bombers. That required suitable aircraft, and the RAF was reluctant to commit valuable bombers to Malta. In May 1939, Pound was recalled to the Admiralty, where he relieved Admiral Blackhouse as First Sea Lord and Admiral of the Fleet. His replacement as commander of the Mediterranean Fleet was Admiral Cunningham, a man who understood the serious threat posed by the Italian battle fleet, and the potential that a naval air strike had to neutralize it. When he took command, he was appraised of the Taranto plan, although by then Captain Lyster had left *Glorious* and was serving as naval ADC to the king. Lyster would return to the Mediterranean only in August 1940, as the rear admiral in charge of the Mediterranean Fleet's carrier force.

The term 'carrier force' is misleading. When Italy entered the war in June 1940, Admiral Cunningham had only one light carrier – *Eagle* – under his command. With a maximum capacity of just two dozen aircraft, *Eagle* was barely large enough to carry out the Taranto attack. *Glorious* had returned to home waters that April, where it was sunk in June, after encountering the German capital ships *Scharnhorst* and *Gneisenau*. To replace it, Cunningham

It was on board the aircraft carrier HMS *Glorious* that the plans for Operation *Judgement* were developed, under the guidance of its commanding officer Captain (later Rear Admiral) Lyster and his senior Fleet Air Arm advisers, while the carrier formed part of the pre-war Mediterranean Fleet.

had been promised the new aircraft carrier *Illustrious*, which was still 'working up' – having its crew become used to their new ship. On 2 September, when it joined the Mediterranean Fleet off Pantellaria, Cunningham finally had the wherewithal to carry out the Taranto operation. Better still, as *Illustrious* was Lyster's flagship, the architect of the plan was in the ideal position to mastermind the attack.

The Admiralty had rejected the original notion of a pre-emptive strike, so what Lyster was left with was an attack on a wartime anchorage, where the defenders would probably be fully prepared. Before the raid could go ahead, both Lyster and Cunningham needed more information on the port's defences, and on the effectiveness of the fleet and the garrison to defend the harbour. To this end Cunningham requested that the RAF conduct a series of aerial reconnaissance flights over Taranto, using aircraft based on Malta.

In September 1940, three RAF Martin Maryland reconnaissance aircraft arrived in Malta. Until then, aerial reconnaissance had been carried out by Short Sunderland flying boats, which had a maximum speed of 200mph and a ceiling of 16,000 feet. They were therefore too slow and vulnerable to risk flying over well-defended Italian ports. By contrast, with a top speed of 278 mph and a ceiling of over 28,000 feet the Marylands were able to carry out their task with ease, and evade any pursuers. From 6 September onwards, these three American-built planes of 431 General Reconnaissance Flight conducted regular sweeps over Taranto, as well as other key Italian ports and airfields. Led by Squadron Leader Whitely, the flight began gathering priceless information on the port's defences, and the movement of Italian warships. Without 431 Flight, the raid on Taranto could never have taken place.

The Fairey Swordfish first flew in 1934, and entered service with the Fleet Air Arm three years later. Nicknamed 'the Stringbag', this combined reconnaissance aircraft, bomber and torpedo plane was both manoeuvrable and reliable, despite its outdated design and limited speed, range and payload.

By late September sufficient reconnaissance photographs had been gathered for Rear Admiral Lyster and his officers to begin planning the attack in fine detail. A date was set – 21 October – the anniversary of the Battle of Trafalgar (1805). Slowly Lyster's team identified the location of the gun batteries and searchlights arrayed around the harbour, as well as the position of anti-torpedo nets, and floating rafts carrying more guns or searchlights. The planners also had to take into account the depth of the water – gleaned from pre-war charts – and the position of man-made obstacles, such as the moles, islands and submerged breakwaters that ringed the Mar Grande. A series of strange blobs mystified the planners, until they were identified as barrage balloons. These would pose a major risk to the airmen, as the torpedo planes would have to fly below the level of the balloons, where at night the wires holding them in place would be invisible. Avoiding them was entirely a matter of luck.

As Trafalgar Day approached the hangar of *Illustrious* was a hub of activity, as 30 Swordfish were readied. Then, two days before the operation, a mechanic slipped, and caused a spark, which resulted in a small explosion. The Swordfish he was working on was torn apart by the blast, and flames spread to nearby aircraft. By the time fire control crews doused the blaze two aircraft had been destroyed, and the rest damaged by the salt water used to extinguish the fire. There was no option but to postpone the attack. While the crew of *Illustrious* stripped and cleaned every aircraft, Admiral Cunningham pondered a new date for the attack. Then, on 28 October, Italy invaded Greece, and the Greeks requested his help. A new date of 30 October was proposed and rejected, as Cunningham's fleet was fully committed escorting convoys of fuel and munitions to Greece and Crete. Eventually, the date was set – the night of 11 November. This time, Operation *Judgement*, as the raid was now called, would go ahead as planned. However, it would now form part of a much larger operation.

ITALIAN DISPOSITIONS

As the commander of the Italian battle fleet, Ammiraglio di Squadra Campioni was reluctant to concentrate all of his battleships in one place. Although the defences of Taranto were impressive, he realized that the presence of *Illustrious* and *Eagle* in the Mediterranean gave the British the ability to launch a carrier-borne strike against his battleships while they lay

Fleet Air Arm crews being briefed before a flying mission. These young men – officers in the case of the Taranto raid – had all been trained in Britain, with the exception of pilots, who usually received their service flying training in Canada. On being posted to a squadron, further 'working up' training was undertaken on Swordfish TBRs before these aircrews joined an operational aircraft carrier. Despite their age, most of the pilots and observers who flew on the Taranto raid were highly experienced aviators, having served together for several months, if not longer.

at anchor. The harbour was also 300 nautical miles from Malta, and 420 nautical miles from the new British airbases on Crete. However, the risk of air attack was deemed low, as any attack from either island would almost certainly be detected before it reached Taranto, and Italian fighters based in Apulia and Calabria could intercept the attackers before they reached his ships. While the presence of the aircraft carriers was more worrying, again a combination of submarine patrols and aerial reconnaissance had proved effective at detecting British naval movements in the central Mediterranean. So, Campioni was reasonably confident any approach by enemy carriers would be detected before a strike could be launched. While Taranto was fairly exposed to attack from the south, it was closer to the naval battle arena around Malta than Naples, and this reduced the risk of the fleet's being caught in confined waters, such as the Strait of Messina, between Italy and Sicily. In other words, Taranto was the ideal place from which to launch an attack on British naval convoys. Therefore that was where the battle fleet needed to be concentrated.

The other reason Taranto was so important to the Italian Navy was a matter of fuel supplies. The stocks of naval fuel oil in Italy were limited, and the transport of oil from North Africa was problematic, thanks to the presence of Malta astride the Italian sea lanes. So, as Taranto was close to the likely arena of action, a fleet based there would use less fuel than one based farther north on the Italian mainland. The base was also well placed to support Italy's operations in Greece, and to cover troop movements across the Adriatic. So, for the time being Campioni and his ships would remain at Taranto. The port's defences were comprehensive and, in the event of a serious threat developing, Campioni expected to have enough warning to put to sea, either to counter British naval movements, or to avoid being caught in port by enemy aircraft. Given the resources at his disposal, it is hard to fault either Campioni, or Ammiraglio di Squadra Riccardi, who commanded the port's defences. After all, a carrier-borne strike against a well-defended enemy port had never been attempted before. There was no reason to expect an attack of this kind to take place – especially one that came without any warning.

OPERATION *MB8*

In the 'Age of Fighting Sail', it was said that command of the Mediterranean Fleet was the most taxing job in the Royal Navy. It required dealing with naval, military and diplomatic factors across the whole region, from the eastern approaches of Gibraltar to the shores of Syria. In 1940 the pressures on Admiral Cunningham were just as weighty, as he dealt with a similar range of factors in the same geographical area. In early November a number of small-scale operations such as the running of convoys, the transit of reinforcements and the resupply of bases all demanded his attention, and the involvement of his fleet. Operation *Judgement* – the raid on Taranto – was just one of these. So, to make the most of his limited resources, he and his planners devised an all-encompassing operation, codenamed *MB8*, which would last for eight days, 5–11 November. This complex operation involved coordinating with Vice-Admiral Somerville in Gibraltar, the Admiralty in London and the Greek authorities in Athens. Essentially, Operation *MB8* was divided into eight distinct smaller-scale operations:

Operation *MB8*, November 1940

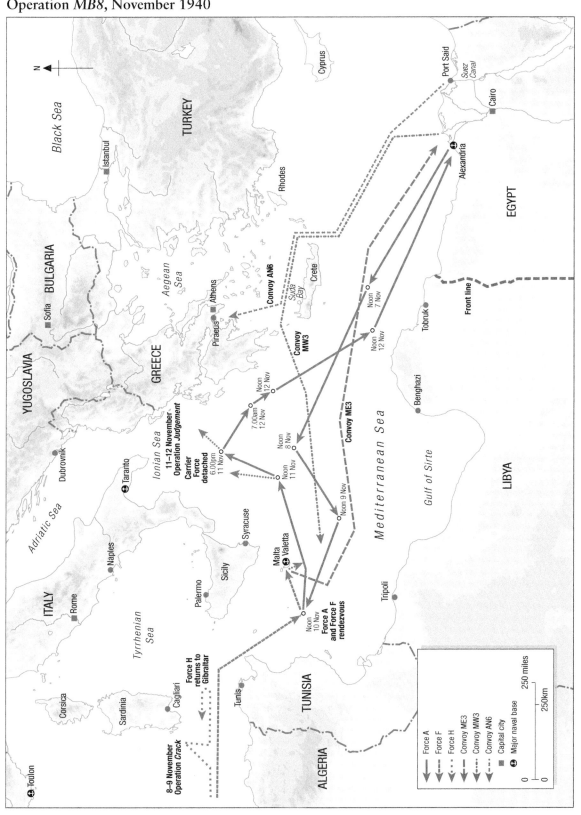

Operation Coat

Reinforcements had been sent out from Britain to join the Mediterranean Fleet. These consisted of the heavy cruiser *Berwick*, the light cruiser *Glasgow* and three destroyers. At Gibraltar they were joined by the battleship *Barham*, which had recently been operating against Vichy French forces off Dakar. A battalion of the Royal East Kent Regiment (the 'Buffs') was then embarked on the battleship – troops earmarked for the defence of Malta. They were to be disembarked in Valetta, before this naval group – Force F – joined up with the Mediterranean Fleet. A fourth destroyer joined the force at Gibraltar before it set sail. Further troops were embarked in the other ships, bringing the total number of soldiers being transported to 2,150.

For its passage to Malta, Force F would be escorted by Vice-Admiral Somerville's Force H. This consisted of his flagship – the aircraft carrier *Ark Royal* – the light cruiser *Sheffield* and eight destroyers. The plan called for Somerville to accompany Force F to a point 165 nautical miles west of Sicily. Before reaching this point around noon on 9 November, *Glasgow* and one destroyer would be temporarily transferred from Force F to Force H. This force would rejoin Force H soon after dawn that morning. Three destroyers would then be detached from Force H, to accompany the rest of Force F as far as Malta. After refuelling, these close escorts would then return to Gibraltar. Before it departed, three Fulmars would be flown off from *Ark Royal*, bound for Malta. These aircraft were reinforcements for *Illustrious*. Before detaching Force H, Somerville would embark on another small operation, codenamed Operation *Crack*.

Operation Crack

Before parting company with Force F, Force H (effectively consisting of *Ark Royal*, *Sheffield*, *Glasgow* and six destroyers) would launch an air strike against the Italian airbase at Cagliari, on the southern coast of Sardinia. This attack, on the morning of 9 November, was designed to disrupt the bomber squadrons based there, and to help ensure the safe passage of the rest of the Operation *Coat* force. This involved a brief detour by Force H during the night of 8–9 November, but Somerville was expected to be back in position protecting Force F before the Italian Air Force launched any air attacks on the British ships. *Glasgow* and its accompanying destroyer would then be handed back to Force F.

Convoy MW3

A convoy of five fully laden merchant ships (Mediterranean Westbound 3) was to sail from Alexandria to Malta. They would be routed around the north of Crete, and for the passage from Alexandria to Suda Bay they would be accompanied by two more merchant ships, carrying supplies for the newly created British base there. The convoy escorts consisted of the AA cruiser *Coventry* and three destroyers. These same escorts would also protect the ships of Convoy AN6 as far as Suda, where this northbound convoy would be detached.

Convoy AN6

This convoy of three tankers and merchant ships (Aegean Northbound 6) would accompany Convoy MW3 and its escorts as far as the north-west coast of Crete. There it would be detached, and head north to Piraeus, where it would unload its cargo. The ships would then return to Suda Bay, before continuing to Alexandria. Their own dedicated escort consisted of the AA cruiser *Calcutta* and two armed trawlers.

Convoy ME3

Four empty merchant ships in Valetta harbour would form a convoy (Mediterranean Eastbound 3), and sail from Malta to Alexandria. Their escorts would consist of the battleship *Ramillies* and a destroyer (detached from Cunningham's main force), and the AA cruiser *Coventry*, which was to be refuelled and sent back to sea after the arrival of Convoy MW3.

Forces B and C

Accompanying Convoy MW3 as far as Crete was Force B – the light cruisers *Sydney* (of the Royal Australian Navy) and *Ajax*, accompanied by two destroyers. They were laden with troops and stores from the Egypt garrison, which would be disembarked at Suda Bay. Meanwhile Force C – the light cruiser *Orion* – laden with RAF stores and equipment, would forge ahead to Suda, and unload its cargo there under cover of darkness. *Orion* would then rejoin Force B off Suda Bay, to create Force X, under the command of Rear Admiral Pridham-Wippell. During 11 November this force would round the Peloponnese and head north towards the Strait of Otranto. There it would conduct a night-time attack on Italian convoys operating between Italy and Greece.

Force A

Meanwhile, Admiral Cunningham in his flagship *Warspite*, accompanied by the battleships *Valiant*, *Malaya* and *Ramillies*, would form the core of the covering force for these operations. It would sail west through the Mediterranean, to take up position to the south-east of Malta. There it would

This reconnaissance photograph of the city of Taranto was taken a few weeks before the Taranto raid, from a Martin Maryland operating from Malta. In this view west is to the top, (1) indicates the commercial harbour, (2) the Canale Navigabile, (3) the Mar Grande, (4) the Mar Piccolo and (5) the torpedo boat quay (Banchina Torpediniere) of the naval dockyard. The latter was the primary target for the bomb-armed Swordfish during the Taranto raid. At the bottom, (6) marks the location of a small dry dock.

be in a position to screen these convoys from attack by the main Italian battle fleet, should it put to sea. The battleship force was accompanied by the aircraft carrier *Illustrious*, the heavy cruiser *York*, the light cruiser *Gloucester*, and eight destroyers or destroyer escorts.

Ramillies and a destroyer would be detached to accompany Convoy MW3 into Malta, where they would then join Convoy ME3. Once Force F reached Malta, they were to disembark their cargo of soldiers, and then put to sea again. After it rendezvoused with Force A to the south-east of Malta, *Illustrious* would be detached, accompanied by the heavy cruisers *Berwick* and *York*, the light cruisers *Gloucester* and *Glasgow*, and four destroyers. *Illustrious* would then carry out Operation *Judgement* – the attack

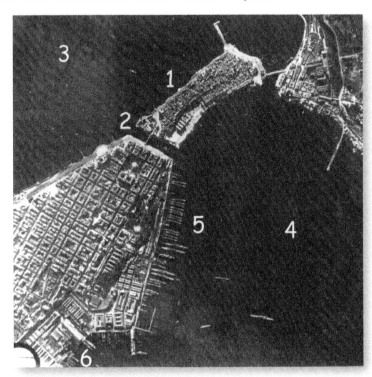

on Taranto. Force A would then withdraw eastwards, covering Convoy ME3, until Rear Admiral Lyster's carrier force and Rear Admiral Pridham-Wippell's cruiser force (Force X) were able to rejoin Cunningham. The combined force would then return to Alexandria.

Operation Judgement

After being detached from Force A, *Illustrious* and its escorts would head north-east, to take up a position to the south-east of the Greek Ionian island Cephalonia. There they would launch their strike against Taranto. Originally, *Eagle* was going to participate in the operation too, but on 5 November it was forced to put in to Alexandria for repairs. However, five aircraft and eight Swordfish crews were transferred from it to *Illustrious*, to boost the size of the strike. During the strike the carrier and its escorts would change location slightly, to reduce the risk of being seen by search aircraft the following morning. After recovering its aircraft *Illustrious*, accompanied by its escorts, would rejoin Cunningham's main fleet.

As for the raid itself, while Lyster's initial plan called for 24 aircraft, only 21 Swordfish were available, including those sent over from *Eagle*. The attack was to have been made in two waves, with 12 aircraft in each. Because of losses, the second wave would now comprise only nine aircraft. Six aircraft in each wave would be armed with torpedoes, while the rest would carry either bombs, or bombs and flares. The bomb-armed aircraft were there to act as a diversion, to confuse the defenders, and to draw attention away from the torpedo-carrying aircraft. This was important, as there were only a limited number of places a successful torpedo attack could be launched from on account of the torpedo nets and moles. The timing of the first strike was also brought forward by an hour to 10.00pm, as Lyster wanted as much time as possible to recover his aircraft and steam out of range of Italian bombers the following morning.

The key to success was surprise. This was why Operation *MB8* actually helped Lyster, as the Italians would be hard pressed to follow all of the complex manoeuvres Cunningham and Somerville had planned during the days preceding the Taranto attack. Until a few hours before the attack, *Illustrious* was tucked away behind the bulk of Cunningham's battle fleet. With luck the Italians would have no inkling a carrier was within striking range of Taranto before it was too late. The most recent reconnaissance photographs of Taranto harbour had been collected from Malta by a Fulmar, and delivered to *Illustrious* the day before Operation *Judgement*. They showed that, in response to the perceived threat of British naval operations in the area, all six battleships of the Italian Navy were now at anchor in Taranto's Mar Grande. Effectively, the harbour was full of suitable targets, making it the perfect time to carry out the long-planned attack. Now it was up to Lyster's aircrews to turn his daring plan into reality.

THE OPERATION

By the morning of 11 November, Admiral Cunningham must have been feeling reasonably content. Despite its complexity, Operation *MB8* had run smoothly. This large-scale enterprise involving two aircraft carriers, five battleships, ten cruisers and 30 destroyers, as well as three distinct convoys, had been planned meticulously; but there was always scope for disaster.

MB8 UNFOLDS

The operation began on 5 November, when the two convoys MW3 and AN6 sailed from Alexandria, accompanied by their escorts. Two days later the ships had reached Suda Bay on the north-west corner of Crete. There Convoy AN6 was detached and headed north into the Aegean, accompanied by *Calcutta*. *Orion* had already steamed on ahead, unloaded its stores for the RAF base at Akrotiri, and was waiting for the convoy as it arrived. The cruisers *Ajax* and *Sydney* unloaded their cargo, and rejoined Pridham-Wippell's flagship as it patrolled the waters to the north. The three cruisers were then designated Force X, and headed west through the Kythira Channel. Pridham-Wippell then continued westwards towards his rendezvous with Admiral Cunningham's main battle fleet.

On 6 November Cunningham in *Warspite* sailed from Alexandria, accompanied by the battleships *Malaya*, *Valiant* and *Ramillies*, the aircraft carrier *Illustrious*, the cruisers *York* and *Gloucester*, and 12 destroyers (*Decoy*, *Defender*, *Hasty*, *Havoc*, *Hereward*, *Hero*, *Hyperion*, *Ilex*, *Janis*, *Jervis*, *Juno* and *Mohawk*). These ships – Force A – headed north-west, and by noon on 7 November they were 80 nautical miles to the south of Crete. Exactly one day later the force reached its next course-changing point, 200 nautical miles due east of Malta. Cunningham now lay directly south of Taranto, in an ideal position to block any attempt by the Italians to intercept the passage of his convoys to Crete and Greece. On hearing that convoys MW3 and AN6 had reached Suda without incident, Force A then headed towards

In this Italian propaganda poster dating from mid-1940 Taranto is highlighted, while the seas around it are ringed by a line of Italian submarines and by the warships of the Italian battle fleet. Troop concentrations and airbases occupy most of the Italian peninsula. To the east of Taranto a minefield spanning the Strait of Otranto protects the Adriatic Sea. The caption, 'Is Italy vulnerable', is answered with a resounding 'No!'

È VULNERABILE L'ITALIA? NO!

The *Andrea Doria* (pictured) and its sister ship *Caio Duilio* were both dreadnoughts launched shortly before World War I, and modernized during the late 1930s. As well as having their main armament altered, the ships were also given a greater degree of underwater protection. This 'Pugliese' system proved ineffective when the *Caio Duilio* was struck by a torpedo during the Taranto raid.

The Fairy Swordfish carried an 18in. Mark XII torpedo, slung beneath its fuselage. To drop it, the Swordfish had to fly level, or with its nose slightly down, at an altitude of 150 feet or less, and at a speed of less than 100mph. The torpedo began running when it struck the water.

the south-west. Meanwhile the remaining five merchant ships of convoy MW3 had followed Pridham-Wippell's cruisers through the Kythira Channel, and were heading towards Malta.

Early on the morning of 7 November Vice-Admiral Somerville's Force H sailed from Gibraltar, accompanied by Force F. Strict security measures were enforced to cover the fact that Force F was acting as a troop convoy, to avoid undue attention from the Italian Air Force. On the evening of 8 November, Somerville in *Ark Royal* detached himself from the rest of the combined force, and headed north, accompanied by *Glasgow*, *Sheffield* and six destroyers. Just before dawn on 9 November nine Swordfish carrying bombs attacked the Italian airbase at Cagliari and caused significant damage to hangars, defences and – most importantly – to the reconnaissance aircraft based there. No British aircraft were lost in the raid. The returning Swordfish were shadowed by an Italian SM-79 'Sparrowhawk', but it was shot down by one of *Ark Royal*'s Fulmars. Three more Fulmars were launched and flew on to Malta, where they would refuel before joining *Illustrious*.

Somerville rejoined Force F before dawn, and his ships formed an anti-aircraft screen around *Ark Royal* and *Barham*. As Somerville's ships approached the point where Force F would be detached, the ships were attacked by 20 Italian SM-79 bombers. The bombs were dropped from a height of 13,000 feet, but although there were several near misses, none of the bombs hit its target. The British ships proceeded on their way, and late on 9 November Force F was detached successfully, when it reached its designated position to the west of the Sicilian Channel. Force F would make this dangerous passage under cover of darkness, and with luck would reach Malta without suffering any more air attacks. Force H then reversed course, and returned to Gibraltar without incident.

Vice-Admiral Somerville later said of the air attack:

They came in one big wave – four sections of five bombers each. Our fighters engaged them as they came in but could not make any visible impression on them. A lot of the pilots were changed when *Ark Royal* was home, and the new lot are still pretty green. Our AA fire as they came over was damned bad, and I was very angry. Of course, this is just an odd collection of ships that have never worked together, so what can you expect.

Fortunately his ships enjoyed one great advantage; the air warning radar fitted to *Ark Royal* gave Somerville advance warning of an air attack, and gave his fighter pilots time to take off and climb to intercept the attackers. Understandably, Somerville ordered that during the passage back to Gibraltar the Force would practise flying combat air patrols and anti-aircraft defence, so that next time they would not let him down.

While Somerville's ships were being attacked, Force A remained undetected, and was now 100 miles to the south-east of Malta. The Italians were certainly trying their best. A picket line of submarines to the south of Sardinia and a patrol of destroyers in the Sicilian Channel failed to locate either Force F or Force H that day, although the Italian Air Force was more successful. The raid on Somerville's ships was launched from airfields in the west of Sicily, 220 nautical miles away to the east, after the British force had been detected by an Italian reconnaissance aircraft. This implied a lack of cooperation between the Italian Air Force and the Navy. A lone Italian submarine – the end of another picket line deployed to the east of Malta – spotted Force A, and fired three torpedoes at *Ramillies*. Despite claims by the captain of the submarine *Capponi*, none of the torpedoes hit the battleship. The submarine was then forced to evade as British destroyers closed in, but it remained undetected. Meanwhile Pridham-Wippell's cruisers had joined Cunningham, and for the next two days would augment the strength of Force A.

The Fulmar crews of *Illustrious* were ready to intercept any approaching enemy bombers, but nothing appeared on the ship's radar. Meanwhile preparations were being made for Operation *Judgement* – the attack on Taranto, which would take place two days later. Unfortunately three aircraft were discovered to have been rendered inoperable as a result of fuel contamination. This reduced the size of the attacking force from 24 to 21 aircraft. Screened by Cunningham's ships, Convoy MW3 was now heading towards Malta, which it would approach from the south during the early hours of 11 November. During the evening of 9 November Cunningham's Force A passed within 25 nautical miles of the island as it steamed towards its rendezvous with Force F. During the night Force F entered the Sicilian Channel, and at noon on 10 November it rendezvoused with Force A near the Italian-held island of Pantelleria. Cunningham remained off Malta for most of the day with this combined force, to screen the nocturnal movement of shipping into and out of Valetta.

During the night of 10–11 November Force F detached itself from Force A again, and made its way to Valetta in Malta to disembark its precious cargo of soldiers. With the exception of the three

When it was completed in May 1940, *Littorio* (pictured) and its sister ship *Vittorio Veneto* became the first Italian battleships to enter service since World War I. Although designed to counter the new French battleships of the Strasbourg class, these two Littorio-class vessels were also more advanced and powerful than the older Queen Elizabeth- and Royal Sovereign-class battleships of the British Mediterranean Fleet.

destroyers borrowed from Force H, the ships put to sea again early on 11 November, and by the early afternoon had rejoined Cunningham to the south of the island. Meanwhile Convoy MW3 also reached Valetta safely, and Convoy ME3 duly put to sea. *Ramillies* and two destroyers had been detached from Force A, to escort MW3 into Valetta. *Ramillies*, *Coventry* and two destroyers were hurriedly refuelled and, after entering port with one convoy, they left it with the other. Owing to its slow speed, *Ramillies* was something of a liability to Cunningham, but it would prove useful as a powerful convoy escort, and its presence in Malta – together with *Barham* – would help boost the morale of the islanders.

Unlike convoy MW3, ME3 would be heading to Alexandria by a more direct route, passing to the south of Crete. It therefore sailed farther to the south-east than the westbound convoy, before altering course to the east for its transit of the eastern Mediterranean. Both the convoys and Force F were fortunate to have avoided air attack during this delicate operation. This, though, was not merely a matter of luck. Fighters from both *Illustrious* and *Malta* had been working hard to screen these movements from Italian reconnaissance aircraft.

Around noon on 11 November Force A was back at its old location, 200 nautical miles east of Malta, which placed Cunningham's ships between Taranto and the eastbound convoy. At that point Pridham-Wippell's Force X was detached from the fleet, and made its own way towards the Strait of Otranto. The three Fulmars sent from *Ark Royal* to Malta had now landed safely on *Illustrious*, and Rear Admiral Lyster and his men were now preparing themselves for their big moment. By 6.00pm Cunningham's ships were in the Ionian Sea, 175 nautical miles to the south-south-east of Taranto. At that point *Illustrious* was detached from Force A, and proceeded towards the north-east, accompanied by its small screen of cruisers and destroyers. Cunningham's remaining ships then turned away, and headed towards the south-east, out of range of Italian bombers based around Taranto. As Rear Admiral Lyster's force detached itself, Cunningham signalled: 'Good luck then, to your lads in their enterprise. Their success may well have a most important bearing on the course of the war in the Mediterranean'. That was the moment when Operation *Judgement* began.

LAUNCHING THE STRIKE

After detaching from Force A, *Illustrious* continued towards the point Lyster had selected as the 'flying off point' for Operation *Judgement*. Designated 'Point X for X-Ray', this position lay 40 nautical miles due west of Kabbo Point on the island of Cephalonia, and 170 nautical miles from Taranto. As the hangar crew fuelled the planes, loaded the ordnance and made their final checks, the aircrews were called into the carrier's wardroom for their final briefing. With 21 Swordfish taking part, that meant a total of 42 pilots and observers were present, together with senior officers, the briefing officer (Commander George Beale) and Lieutenant Commander Opie USN, who was there to observe the operation in an unofficial capacity. Opie had actually been on board *Illustrious* since its working-up period in the West Indies, and was a popular addition to the wardroom. Beale was the ship's operations officer, and although the aircrews were already well briefed, he felt some points needed to be underlined again.

The arrival in Malta of three Martin Maryland reconnaissance aircraft played a vital part in Operation *Judgement*. Unlike the large seaplanes then being used in the reconnaissance role, the Marylands had the speed and ceiling needed to take photographs of Taranto without incurring a high risk of being shot down by Italian fighters.

A reconnaissance photograph of the battleship anchorage at the eastern side of Taranto's Mar Grande, taken on 10 November 1940. In this photograph, showing all six Italian battleships in the anchorage, south is at the top. They were still in the same position the following evening, when the Fleet Air Arm carried out its attack.

Beale stood on a chair to address the men as he outlined the plan. Lieutenant Commander Williamson would lead the first wave of 12 Swordfish, and would take off at 8.30pm. The aircraft would launch at ten-second intervals, and form up on Williamson's plane. The wave would then fly directly towards Taranto, which lay to the north-west. Six of the aircraft would carry torpedoes, while four (flown by Patch, Forde, Murray and Sarra) carried bombs. The final two (flown by Kiggell and Lamb) carried a mixture of bombs and incendiary flares. The flare droppers would lead the way, and drop their flares on the eastern side of the Mar Grande. This would then illuminate the battleships for the torpedo bombers, who would approach the anchorage from the west. The flare droppers would then drop their bombs around the dock facilities and oil storage depot to the east of the anchorage, while the remaining three Swordfish would bomb targets of opportunity in the Mar Piccolo. The second wave of nine Swordfish led by Lieutenant Commander Hale would take off at 9.20pm, and the five torpedo planes would

Operation *Judgement*, November 1940

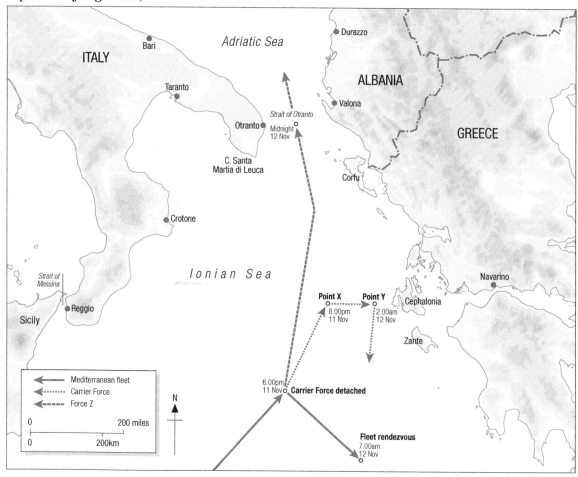

approach the Mar Piccolo from the north-west – actually flying over the city – after two flare-dropping planes (flown by Hamilton and Skelton) had dropped their incendiary flares in the same location as those of the first strike. Meanwhile the remaining two bomb-armed Swordfish (flown by Clifford and Morford) would attack ships in the Mar Piccolo.

Beale emphasized that the torpedoes were all fitted with the new Duplex warhead. These were designed to explode beneath the target, whether it hit the ship or not. The torpedoes were set to pass beneath the Italian torpedo nets, and approach their targets at a depth of around 35 feet. Beale then reminded the men of the location of the Italian barrage balloons and torpedo nets, and the known anti-aircraft emplacements. He stressed that complete radio silence would be maintained throughout the operation. The only exception was the signal 'Attack Completed', which was to be sent to *Illustrious* by the wave leader, after each of the two attacks had been completed. When he turned his attention to the return journey, one airman quipped, 'Don't let's bother about that'! This produced some forced chuckles, but it underlined that for many of the men in the wardroom, they expected this would be a one-way mission. Nevertheless, Beale described the course of the return leg, and the location of the waiting aircraft carrier.

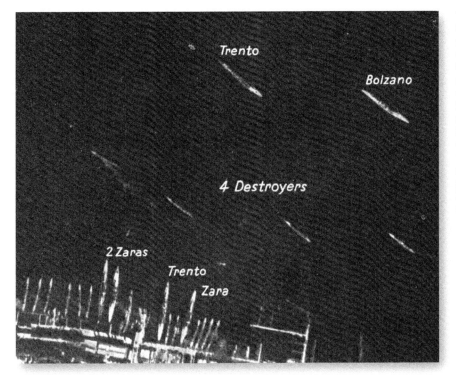

Taken on 10 November, this British aerial reconnaissance photograph shows the position of six Italian heavy cruisers in the Mar Piccolo, either berthed stern first against the quayside of the naval dockyard, or lying farther out, behind a line of anchored destroyers. The *Trento* had moved away from the quayside by the time the raid took place, while the two Zara-class cruisers marked on the photograph were actually two light cruisers of the Abruzzi class.

Then, Rear Admiral Lyster addressed the men, saying simply, 'Go to it, and good luck'.

The men then studied the aerial photographs and the chart, and talked quietly among themselves, drinking coffee and smoking cigarettes. Shortly before 8.00pm the men of the first wave donned their flying gear of Sidcup flying suits and 'Mae West' lifejackets, and made their way to the flight deck. From 8.10pm onwards they clambered into their aircraft, and the fitters helped them strap on their Sutton harnesses and parachute straps. The pilots then conducted their own last-minute checks on their aircraft, and readied themselves for the launch. Meanwhile the observers arrayed their Bigsworth chart tables, their navigational instruments and their binoculars, before checking the radios they were forbidden to use. Then they waited.

Their 12 planes were already ranged on deck, in a staggered formation, with Williamson's aircraft at the front. All of the engines were started. By then Captain Boyd, the commander of *Illustrious*, was at Point X, and had turned the carrier into the wind, and increased speed to 28 knots. This meant that the wind was whipping across the flight deck at a little over 30mph. This would help the laden Swordfish reach their take-off speed as quickly as possible, and climb into the air. Finally, at 8.30pm precisely, Commander Robertson flashed his green Aldis lamp – the signal to proceed. Williamson gunned his aircraft, and signalled to the flight deck crew. The chocks were whipped away from the wheels, and Swordfish L4A began rolling forward. Williamson pushed his throttle forward and the aircraft lifted from the deck. Behind it, Swordfish L4K flown by Lieutenant Kemp, the senior pilot of 815 Squadron was already moving. One after the other the 12 Swordfish of the first wave roared forward and took off. By 8.40pm all the aircraft were airborne. The long-planned raid was now under way.

THE FIRST WAVE

First wave (Lt. Cdr. Williamson)

Swordfish (ordnance carried)	Squadron	Pilot	Observer	Note
L4A (1 torpedo)	815	Lt. Cdr. K. Williamson	Lt. N. Scarlett	Shot down, crew survived
L4C (1 torpedo)	815	S/Lt. P. D. Sparke	S/Lt. A. L. Neale	
L4R (1 torpedo)	815	S/Lt. A. Macaulay	S/Lt. A. Wray	
L4K (1 torpedo)	815	Lt. N. Kemp	Lt. G. W. Bailey	
L4M (1 torpedo)	815	Lt. H. Swayne	S/Lt. J. Buscall	
L4P (16 flares, 4 bombs)	815	Lt. L. J. Kiggell	Lt. H. Janvrin	
L5B (16 flares, 4 bombs)	819	Lt. C. Lamb	Lt. K. Grieve	
L4L (6 bombs)	815	S/Lt. W. C. Sarra	Mid. J. Barker	
L4H (6 bombs)	815	S/Lt. A. Forde	S/Lt. A. Mardel-Ferreira	
E4F (1 torpedo)	813	Lt. M. Maund	S/Lt. W. Bull	
E5A (6 bombs)	824	Capt. O. Patch RM	Lt. D. Goodwin	
E5Q (6 bombs)	824	Lt. J. Murray	S/Lt. S. Paine	

Note: the prefix 'E' designated an aircraft from *Eagle*, 'L' from *Illustrious*.

Eight nautical miles from *Illustrious*, Williamson eased back on his throttle, and waited for the rest of the wave to catch him up. They formed up into four flights of three aircraft each. Once the aircraft reached him, Williamson banked and set a course towards Taranto. Communication between planes was not possible owing to the imposition of radio silence, so hand gestures or Morse code signals sent by signal lamp had to suffice. Communication within the plane was not easy either, as it was via a primitive speaking tube linking the pilot and observer's cockpits. If the observer wanted to speak, he would tap the pilot on the shoulder, and both men would pick up the voice pipe. If the pilot wanted to initiate a conversation, he would rock his wings. Normally a Swordfish had a crew of three – the third member being a gunner and radio operator. For the raid this third crew member was dispensed with, to allow the aircraft to carry a long-range fuel tank. On torpedo-carrying aircraft, these were attached to the observer's cockpit using metal straps. For the bombers, they were slung beneath the fuselage.

The plan called for the aircraft to climb to an altitude of 6,000 feet for their journey to Taranto. Flying time was a little over two hours and 20 minutes, at their assigned cruising speed of 75mph. However, after approximately an hour, the aircraft encountered thick cloud at that altitude, and Williamson followed the standing instructions to climb above it. At 7,500 feet Williamson and his observer Scarlett broke through the clouds, and minutes later they were joined by eight other aircraft. Four more – one carrying torpedoes and three armed with bombs – had become lost in the clouds. Williamson loitered for a little, and then signalled to the others to press on. They formed up into flights again, and continued their journey towards Taranto. The others would simply have to catch up as best they could.

Lieutenant Maund in E4F later remembered how cold it was flying in the clouds, before recalling the problems he had catching up with the others in the darkness: 'I see formation lights ahead, and climb after them, following them through one of the rare holes in this cloud mass. There are two aircraft sure enough, yet when I range up alongside, the moon's glow shows up the figure "5A" – that is Olly (Patch). The others must be ahead. After an anxious few minutes, some dim lights appear amongst the upper billows of the cloud, and opening the throttle we lumber away from Olly after them. Poor old engine – it will be getting a tanning this trip'. They still had 40 minutes to go before they reached their objective.

The pilots whose aircraft became lost in the fog made their own way to Taranto, guided by the navigational instructions of their observers. One of these teams – Swayne and Buscall in L4M, actually reached Taranto well ahead of the other aircraft of the wave, and loitered several miles to seaward of the port for 15 minutes, before the others caught up. It was later claimed that the anti-aircraft fire that erupted around Taranto at 10.50pm that night was triggered by a reconnaissance flight by a Short Sunderland flying boat from 228 Squadron of the RAF. In all probability, the firing was initiated by the arrival of Swordfish L4M. That evening, a reconnaissance plane had indeed been detected flying over the Gulf of Taranto, but that was shortly before 8.00pm, and although the port's air raid warning had sounded, the alarm was cancelled 45 minutes later, and the port's AA crews stood down from their action stations. Still, it showed that the listening stations around Taranto were effective, and their operators were doing their job.

At 10.45pm more engine noises were heard – the approach of Swayne and Buscall – and the alarm was sounded for the second time that evening. Five minutes later the port's AA guns began firing a flak barrage, even though no aircraft had been spotted. Again, L4M had been detected by the listening posts, but was loitering out of harm's way. The barrage certainly helped the other 11 aircraft of the first wave to locate the port. A few minutes later Williamson sighted Taranto ahead of him, beneath the flak bursts, and at 10.56pm he signalled to the other aircraft of his wave to break formation. The aircraft split up into groups, depending on what task they had been assigned during the attack.

The first in position were the two flare-dropping planes, L4P crewed by Kiggell and Janvrin, and L5B, crewed by Lamb and Grieve. The others waited just outside the port until these two planes had made their approach from the south. They flew over the headland of the Capo San Vito at 8,000 feet, and dropped their flares in a line, running north-eastwards along the south-eastern side of the Mar Grande. The shore there was lined by barrage balloons, and the two pilots made sure to keep out of their way by keeping the balloons to their left. Maund described the effect: 'A burst of brilliance on the north-eastern [actually south-eastern] shore, and then another and another as the flare-dropper releases his load, until the harbour shows clear in the light he has made. Not too bright to dull the arc of raining colour over the harbour where tracer flies, allowing, it seems, no room to escape unscathed.'

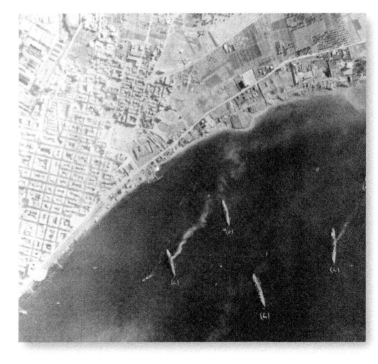

The battleship anchorage in the Mar Grande, pictured a few days before the attack. Five battleships can be seen in this photograph – identified as (C) for Cavour class or (L) for Littorio class by the RAF analyst. In fact two of the (C) battleships are Andrea Doria-class vessels – the *Caio Duilio* on the left of the photograph, and the *Andrea Doria* on the right. The remaining (C) battleship is the *Giulio Cesare*, moored astern of the *Littorio*. Its sister ship, the *Conti di Cavour*, is not visible in this photograph.

LAUNCH OF THE FIRST WAVE FROM HMS *ILLUSTRIOUS* (PP. 54–55)

Shortly before 8.30pm on 11 November, the aircraft carrier *Illustrious* has reached 'Point X' – the position chosen by Rear Admiral Lyster from which to launch the air strike on Taranto. The Italian port lay 189 nautical miles to the north-west. The carrier group turns into the wind for the launch, and increases speed to 30 knots. On board *Illustrious* the 12 aircraft of the first wave have already been ranged on the after end of the flight deck **(1)** in 'herringbone' formation, and are ready for take-off. At 8.30pm precisely a green lamp is flashed from the bridge **(2)**, and the leading Swordfish piloted by Lt. Cdr. Williamson speeds down the flight deck and takes off. The other aircraft follow at 10-second intervals. Of the dozen aircraft in the first wave, six are armed with torpedoes, four with bombs, and two with a mixture of bombs and flares. In this view the Swordfish in the foreground **(3)** is the third to take off. It is aircraft L4R, crewed by Sub. Lt. Macaulay (pilot) and Sub. Lt. Wray (observer), both from *Illustrious*' 815 Squadron. Usually a Swordfish had a crew of three, but for this mission, because an extra fuel tank was mounted over the observer's position in torpedo-armed planes, the rear gunner was left behind, and his seat occupied by the observer instead. All of 815 Squadron's Swordfish have a darkened lower fuselage, as they have been repainted using distemper for night flying missions. The remaining Swordfish which took part in the raid retained the lighter lower fuselage and lower wing colour of light blue-grey. Below them **(4)** the fourth aircraft – L4K, crewed by lieutenants Kemp and Bailey – has just taken off, while in the centre of the flight deck **(5)** L4M is just about to begin its take-off run. Both of these aircraft are armed with a single torpedo. One of the carrier's escorts, the heavy cruiser *York* **(6)** can be seen, keeping station off the port beam of *Illustrious*. The four cruisers are stationed ahead, astern and on either beam of the carrier, while the four destroyers take up positions between each pair of cruisers, to form an eight-ship cordon around the carrier.

Janvrin, the observer to Kiggell in L4P wrote:

> We had a grandstand view, as we didn't go down to sea level. We dropped our flares at about 8,000 feet … and in fact we were fired at considerably. We had a fair amount of ack-ack fire [flak], and most extraordinary things that looked like flaming onions – one just sort of went through it, and it made no great impression. One didn't think that they would ever hit you – there was always fear but I think in the same way that one has butterflies in the tummy beforehand, but when things are actually happening you don't seem to notice the butterflies much.

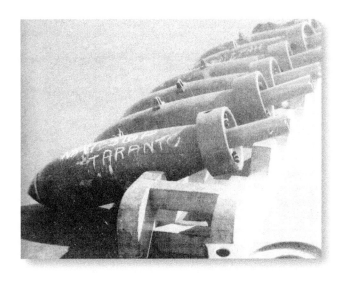

Before the raid, the crew of *Illustrious* took the liberty of chalking messages onto several of the bombs and torpedoes which would be carried on the mission. These 250lb semi-armour-piercing (SAP) bombs would all be dropped during the raid.

His Swordfish was the first to make its run – L5B held back, loitering at 5,000 feet until the first Swordfish was clear. They then followed it in, climbing slightly before dropping their own flares in the same area. Their timing was perfect – the first of these flares burst into a yellow ball of light just as the first torpedo-carrying Swordfish began its approach over the Mar Grande.

Their job done, the two flare-dropping planes then chose suitable targets in the area for their bombs. Both chose the oil storage depot that lay about a mile inland from the harbour, and which was connected to the Mar Grande by a pipeline, terminating in a refuelling pier. Both L4P and L5B dropped four bombs each on the target, then headed for home, their job done for the evening. Behind them they left the oil depot burning fiercely. Before they left, Kiggell and Janvrin were able to see the start of the attack made by the torpedo-carrying planes.

The first three aircraft – Williamson and Scarlett in L4A, Macaulay and Wray in L4R and Sparke and Neale in L4C – all dropped altitude before reaching the harbour, and swept low over the island of San Pietro, which marked the outer boundary of the Mar Grande. To reach their targets, all three aircraft had to cross the breakwater known as the Diga di Tarantola, which was lined with barrage balloons. The balloons themselves were not a problem – the danger was posed by the wires that tethered them in place. In the darkness the cables were completely invisible, and the aircrews later

This painting by wartime naval artist Lieutenant Rowland Langmaid RN is entitled '*Illustrious* parts company with the 3rd CS (Cruiser Squadron), for attack on Taranto', and shows the moment when Rear Admiral Lyster's force parted company with the rest of the Mediterranean Fleet, on the afternoon of 11 November.

claimed that they never saw the cables during the attack. They knew they were there though, and could only hope they would not run into them. Williamson and Scarlett were the first to pass through the line of cables. Once through, the battleships lay before them. The ships were firing now, and between the plane and their target lay two destroyers – *Lampo* and *Fulmine*. They dropped to 30 feet, flying through a wall of machine-gun fire from the destroyers, and saw

Map labels: SUBMERGED BREAKWATER · ISLA SAN PIETRO · AA (ANTI-AIRCRAFT BATTERIES) · SUBMERGED BREAKWATER · ISOLETTO SAN PAOLO · DIGA D SAN VIT · C. SAN VITO

EVENTS

1. 11.10pm: Swordfish L4P (Kiggell & Janvrin) drops to the east of the barrage balloons lining the eastern side of the Mar Piccolo.

2. 11.12pm: Swordfish L4A (Williamson & Scarlett) begins its attack on the *Caio Duilio*, passing through the barrage balloon cables along the Diga di Tarantola to emerge in the battleship anchorage.

3. 11.14pm: Williamson & Scarlett in L4A sweep past Italian destroyers and release their torpedo, aiming it at the *Conti di Cavour*. Moments later the low-flying plane is hit, and crashes into the harbour to the south of the battleship. Their torpedo detonates against the port side of the battleship. Both British crewmen survive the crash, and are subsequently rescued and taken prisoner.

4. 11.15pm: Sparke & Neale in L4C and Macauley and Wray in L4R originally intended to attack the *Vittorio Veneto*, but found they did not have a clear shot. They launch at the *Conti di Cavour* instead, but both torpedoes miss their target.

5. 11.16pm: Swordfish L4M (Swayne & Buscall) in the second group of aircraft flies around the southern end of the line of raft-mounted barrage balloons blocking the path, and begin an attack run on the *Littorio*. Its torpedo strikes the battleship on its port side.

6. 11.16pm: in Swordfish L4K Kemp & Bailey also select the *Littorio*, having skirted around the northern end of the line of barrage balloons. The torpedo strikes the battleship on its starboard side.

7. 11.18pm: the sixth torpedo-carrying plane, E4F (Maund & Bull) follows the northern edge of the Mar Grande as it makes its approach, and then selects the *Littorio* as its target. The torpedo misses it, but is on course to hit the *Vittorio Veneto* behind. However, it buries itself in the seabed before reaching the battleship.

8. 11.16–11.26pm: E5A (Patch & Goodwin), L4H (Forde & Mardel-Ferreira) and E5Q (Murray & Paine) are unable to locate the heavy cruisers in the Mar Piccolo, so attack a line of smaller warships moored along the quayside on the southern edge of the inner harbour. Although one destroyer might have been hit, no significant damage is caused.

9. 11.30pm: in Swordfish L4L, Sarra & Barker also fail to locate the enemy cruisers that are their primary targets, so instead they release their bombs over a seaplane base. One explodes inside a hangar, causing a fire and destroying two aircraft.

10. 11.34pm: the two flare-dropping planes circle around and launch a bombing attack on the Italian Navy's oil storage depot, to the south-east of the Mar Grande. A number of hits are scored, before the aircraft – L4P and L5B – head away from Taranto, thereby bringing the attack to a close.

THE ATTACK ON TARANTO – THE FIRST WAVE, 11.10–11.35PM, 11 NOVEMBER 1940

Shortly before 11.00pm, as his 12 Swordfish in the wave approach Taranto from the south, Lt. Cdr. Williamson gives the order to begin the attack. Two of the aircraft carry flares, four carry bombs and the remaining six are torpedo bombers.

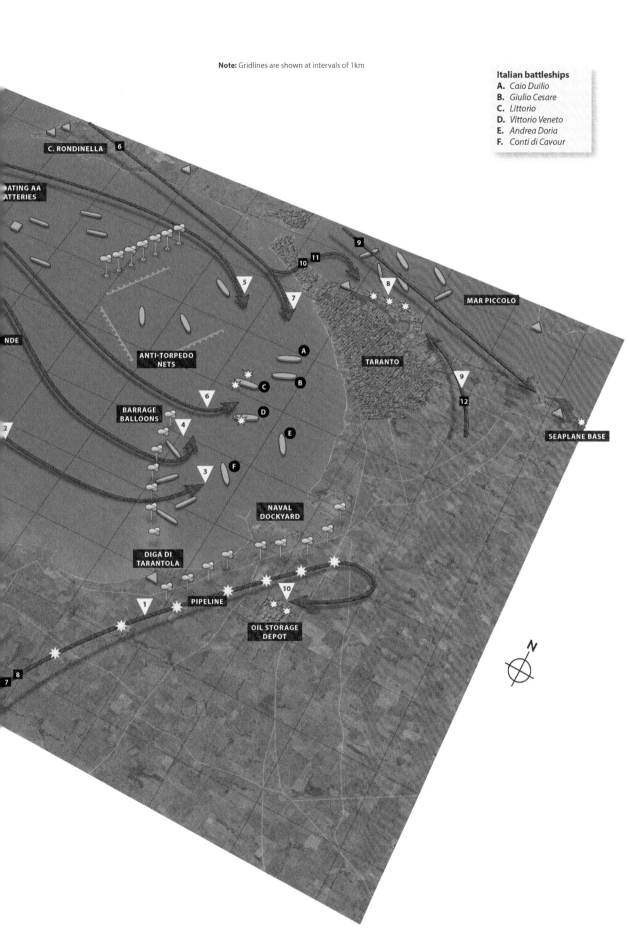

Note: Gridlines are shown at intervals of 1km

Italian battleships
A. Caio Duilio
B. Giulio Cesare
C. Littorio
D. Vittorio Veneto
E. Andrea Doria
F. Conti di Cavour

C. RONDINELLA

FLOATING AA
BATTERIES

ANTI-TORPEDO
NETS

BARRAGE
BALLOONS

TARANTO

MAR PICCOLO

SEAPLANE BASE

NAVAL
DOCKYARD

DIGA DI
TARANTOLA

PIPELINE

OIL STORAGE
DEPOT

N

the battleship *Conti di Cavour* moored ahead of them. They were approaching it from its beam – a perfect firing angle. They released their torpedo, and turned towards the centre of the harbour, to avoid the worst of the flak.

That was when disaster struck. Scarlett could not tell if they crashed because of being hit, or because of some other problem. He recalled: 'We put a wingtip in the water. I couldn't tell. I just fell out of the back into the sea. We were only about 20 feet up – it wasn't very far to drop. I never tie myself in on those occasions.' He surfaced, and looked around, 'then old Williamson came up a bit later, and we hung about by the aircraft which had its tail sticking out of the water. Chaps ashore were shooting at it. The water was boiling [due to enemy fire], so I swam off to a floating dock and climbed aboard that. We didn't know if we'd done any good with our torpedo.' In fact their torpedo had struck the battleship amidships on its port side, and it immediately began to sink. Williamson recalled swimming away from the aircraft through rain, then realizing the drops on the water were caused by bullets. They spent about half an hour clinging to the tail of their Swordfish before making for the relative safety of the floating dock. While most of the bullets were probably not aimed at them but at other aircraft, they were lucky to survive the experience.

Macaulay and Wray in L4R approached the battleships behind Sparke and Neale in L4C, hoping to minimize the risk of hitting one of the balloon cables. Both Swordfish passed through the barrier, and found themselves a little to the north of Williamson. They passed between the destroyers *Lampo* and *Belena*, and saw the explosion caused by Williamson and Savage's torpedo hit on *Conti di Cavour* ahead and to their right. Both pilots had intended to attack the fleet flagship – the battleship *Vittorio Veneto* – but it was bow on to them, and at an awkward angle on their port beam. Instead they fired at the *Conti di Cavour*. Both torpedoes missed the target, but ran on across the harbour, to detonate close to the *Andrea Doria*, which was beam on to the torpedoes, and approximately 1,500 yards from their launching point. However, neither torpedo caused any damage. After releasing their torpedoes the two Swordfish banked to port, and made their exit, using the island of San Pietro as their guide as they headed away from the anchorage.

HMS *Illustrious* pictured under way, with its transmitting masts lowered, ready for flying operations. In order to launch or recover its aircraft, *Illustrious* – and its escorts – had to alter course into the wind, and increase speed, to maximize the airflow over its flight deck.

It was now the turn of the second sub-flight. Its lead plane was L4K, crewed by Kemp and Bailey. Like the two other aircraft of the sub-flight – E4F and L4M – they were to attack the battleships from the north-west. Kemp and Bailey flew low over the line of the submerged breakwater leading from the mainland to the island of San Pietro, and followed the curve of the harbour, trying to keep clear of the destroyers and cruisers that lay between them and the battleship anchorage. Another obstacle in their path was a line of barrage balloons tethered to rafts, which they had studied on the aerial photographs and hoped to avoid by their indirect route. It worked. They bypassed the line of balloons and passed to the north of the cruiser anchorage, where the heavy cruisers *Fiume* and *Zara* were adding their weight of fire to the flak. Then they spotted the battleships lying at their moorings – the *Caio Diulio* to their left, and the brand-new *Littorio* to their right. Both battleships were almost beam on – making the Swordfish well placed to launch its attack. They selected the *Littorio*, and dropped their torpedo. Kemp saw its streak of bubbles as he banked away to starboard. He climbed steeply as he did so, trying to clear the line of barrage balloons lining the Diga di Tarantola, which lay ahead of him. His torpedo struck the battleship on its starboard side, and it immediately began listing.

Unlike their companions in L4K, Swayne and Buscall in L4M decided to skirt the destroyers, cruisers and line of barrage balloon-carrying rafts by flying to the south of them, across the centre of the Mar Grande. The Swordfish crossed the breakwater at 1,000 feet, and then lost altitude during the approach. As he flew across the harbour, Swayne noticed two things. First, most of the flak was being fired over their heads. Secondly, no searchlights were being used. If they had been, he doubted whether he or any of the other airmen would have survived. They reached the battleship anchorage at a height of a little under 100 feet. They passed just north of the mole, and then Swayne banked hard to port. Ahead of him lay the *Littorio*, lying beam on.

Essentially Swayne and Buscall were approaching the battleship from the opposite side from Kemp and Bailey, and almost at the same time. They released their torpedo 400 yards from the battleship's starboard side, and then banked sharply to port again, to reach the outer side of the harbour. They left it late though, and Swayne actually flew over the battleship, climbing hard to clear it. The Swordfish flew between the battleship's masts before it could turn away to port. In the process of evading the battleships they passed close to the heavy cruiser *Gorizia*, the guns of which were firing haphazardly to both port and starboard. They roared past it, gaining altitude as they did so, and headed for the submerged breakwater and the open sea. As the plane swept over the *Littorio*, Buscall in the observer's cockpit thought he saw a column of smoke below him.

Swordfish E4F was crewed by Maund and Bull. It was the last torpedo-carrying plane of the wave, and reached the Mar Grande by flying over the headland of Capo Rondinello, where the submerged breakwater joined the mainland. Its flight path lay close to the houses and gardens of the western portion of the city itself, which the pilot raced over at 1,000 feet. He gradually dropped his altitude to 100 feet, and checked his location against a recognizable landmark – a large factory chimney. When

A Fairey Swordfish being prepared for flight. When in the hangar or otherwise not in use, its wings were folded back to reduce the space the large aircraft took up. These had to be manually folded out and locked in place. In this photograph the pylons used to mount bombs can be clearly seen on the underside of its wing.

ATTACK OF THE FIRST WAVE ON THE BATTLESHIP ANCHORAGE AT TARANTO (PP. 62–63)

At 11.12pm on the evening of 11 November 1940 the 12 Swordfish of the first wave begin their attack. While the six torpedo-armed aircraft will make torpedo attacks on the battleships moored in the Mar Grande, those Swordfish armed with bombs will attack targets of opportunity in the nearby Mar Piccolo. Just before the torpedo aircraft make their run the two remaining Swordfish are scheduled to drop parachute flares just beyond the south-east shore of the Mar Grande. The aim is to make the targets easier to see for the attacking aircraft. The battleships are protected by anti-torpedo nets, lines of barrage balloons, and anti-aircraft batteries. When the attack begins, three of the Swordfish launch attacks on targets in the northern part of the battleship anchorage, and three approach the battleship anchorage over the breakwater at its southern edge. To the north lie the battleships *Caio Duilio*, *Giulio Cesare* and *Littorio*. This plate though, captures the scene during the attack by the leading plane, which approaches the anchorage from the south-west. The battleship *Conte di Cavour* (1) can be seen in the middle distance, laying down a barrage of anti-aircraft fire at the approaching aircraft. Behind it, off its starboard bow lie the battleships *Vittorio Veneto* (2) and *Andrea Doria* (3). These stationary battleships are silhouetted by the glow of the parachute flares (4) dropped behind the ships by L4P, one of the two flare-carrying Swordfish. In the foreground is Swordfish L4A (5), piloted by the strike leader, Lt. Cdr. Williamson. His observer is Lt. Scarlett. They approach the battleship anchorage by flying through the barrage balloon cables over the Diga di Tarantola breakwater, and pass over a cluster of destroyers before beginning their torpedo run. *Conti di Cavour* lies dead ahead of them, beam on to the aircraft – the perfect angle for an attack. However, a wall of anti-aircraft fire (6) is directed at them from the battleship and from other vessels in the harbour – most of the shore-based anti-aircraft fire flies above their heads. Williamson releases his torpedo at a range of around 640 yards, and a height of 30 feet (7). Moments later L4A is hit, and crashes into the harbour. Although the plane is lost, both crewmen survive, and are taken prisoner. The torpedo scores a direct hit on the battleship, which founders in the shallow water of the harbour.

he drew level with the canal leading from the Mar Grande to the Mar Piccolo he began turning to starboard, towards the battleship anchorage. Like the other aircraft of his flight he spotted the *Littorio*, lying ahead of him, beam on. He dropped lower, as a wall of flak flew over the plane, fired from the cruisers to his right-hand side. Fire was also coming from behind him, where more gun batteries protected the canal. Maund hoped that by banking the plane to starboard he would temporarily throw off the gunners' aim.

He then lined up on his target, visible as a dark shape ahead of him. Because of the heavy fire he decided to launch his torpedo as soon as he could. He dropped his torpedo at a range of 1,300 yards, and held his course until he could see it hit the water, and then waited until he could see the trail of bubbles that meant it was powering its way to the target. He then banked sharply to starboard, dodging past the Italian cruisers below him as he made his escape. He thought he was clear of danger when he saw a destroyer ahead of him, its pom-pom gun level with his cockpit. It was probably the *Gioberti*, and for some reason the Italian gunners did not open fire, probably because they were already out of ammunition. Maund turned away, and headed for San Pietro Island, zigzagging as he went, with lines of tracer chasing him. The plane eventually reached the open sea, and Maund banked and climbed. He risked a look back, and exclaimed to Bull, 'My Christ, Bull! Just look at that bloody awful mess! Just look at it!' He had caught a glimpse of battleships on fire in the inner harbour, and flak flying everywhere. He then set an easterly course for home.

While the torpedo-carrying aircraft were making their approach, the bomb-carrying Swordfish approached the Mar Piccolo. The idea was that they would attack just after the first flares had been dropped, but before the torpedo planes made their run, to maximize the confusion about what was happening. There were four bomb-carrying Swordfish in this sub-flight, led by Captain Patch of the Royal Marines in E5A, with Goodwin as his observer, a man who often took a chamber pot with him when flying. The other three aircraft in the group were L4L, crewed by Sarra and Barker, L4H, crewed by Forde and Mardel-Ferreira, and finally Murray and Paine in E5Q. It was Patch and Goodwin who led the attack, crossing San Pietro Island at 8,500 feet, and heading across the Mar Grande towards the canal leading to the Mar Piccolo. From studying the aerial photographs the bomber pilots knew that the main warship anchorage in the Mar Piccolo lay a little to the east of the canal, where three heavy cruisers and a cluster of destroyers swung at their moorings.

This Fleet Air Arm diagram explains how, by sailing into the wind and increasing the ship's speed, the air speed over the flight deck is increased, which provides additional lift to the aircraft. This in turn means that the aircraft can take off at a slower speed and in a shorter distance than would otherwise be the case.

Patch noticed that the flak barrage intensified as they approached the city – he later described it as 'the wonderful Brock's firework display' – Brock's being a popular British firework manufacturer. They were unable to see the cruisers as they made their approach, their plane buffeted by flak bursts, as the south side of the Mar Piccolo seemed to be in shadow. They spent two minutes circling over the town before they spotted the cruisers. Two of them lay at their moorings, while a third seemed to be berthed alongside a pontoon, sticking out at right angles from the main quayside. Behind them the quay itself was lined with smaller Italian warships. Then the ships spotted them, and opened fire, their tracer fire arching upwards towards the circling biplane. However, without searchlights Patch was fairly confident that they were firing blind.

All this time he had been losing altitude, and so E5A was now 1,500 feet above the surface of the inner harbour. He banked sharply, and put the plane into a dive. Swordfish do not make ideal dive-bombers – their folding wings are too fragile – so the attack was not a classic dive-bombing run, but more of a shallow dive. Patch aimed for the line of smaller ships berthed stern on to the quayside. He flattened out and dropped his six bombs, one of which had a black marine boot tied to it – an additional gift from the Royal Marines. Tracer was streaming all around the plane, but amazingly it remained unscathed. After dropping his bombs Patch banked to port, exclaimed, 'Thank God that's over' to Goodwin, and then turned away to the east to avoid the flak. Goodwin tried to look back to see what damage had been done, but his vision was hampered by a bright blaze centred on the seaplane base, just to the east of the quay.

That blaze was the work of Sarra and Barker in L4L. Their Swordfish had approached Taranto from the west, flying over the mainland at 8,000 feet to reach the Mar Piccolo, where Sarra dived to 1,500 feet. Like Patch a few seconds earlier, Sarra had been unable to spot any of the cruisers – his assigned target – so he flew over the dockyard and its quayside, which ran along the southern shore of the inner harbour. The eastern portion of the city lay on the plane's right-hand side. He still could not see much, but then he spotted the seaplane base directly ahead of him. This small complex of hangars, fuel and ammunition dumps and slipways would make an excellent alternative target. He knew it would be well defended, but the anti-aircraft fire was already intense, as both the shore-based AA batteries and the guns of the warships to his left were all firing blindly into the air. Like Patch he reckoned they would have a hard job spotting the plane without switching on searchlights.

He dropped his bombs from 500 feet, and glimpsed one fall through the roof of a hangar, causing a large explosion. Other bombs seemed to land

In this contemporary aerial view of Taranto the Mar Grande can be seen on the right, surrounded by the same islands and curving submerged breakwaters that delineated it in 1940. The Mar Piccolo is in the foreground, while the canal joining the inner and outer harbours is also clearly visible.

around the slipways, and beside other buildings. The bombing seemed to spur the base's defensive batteries into action, and tracer began creeping towards the plane. Sarra banked away to starboard and headed towards the south-east. Like Patch he opted to fly over the Puglian heel of Italy, rather than reach the open sea by flying back over the city or outer harbour. During the flight to Taranto, Forde and Mardel-Ferreira in L4H had lost contact with the rest of the sub-

flight, but had linked up with Williamson and his torpedo bombers. They followed them towards the Italian base, and arrived off the southern side of the Mar Grande at the same time as Kiggell and Janvrin in L4P began dropping their parachute flares. Forde roared over the coast near Capo San Vito, and flew along the western side of the flares, avoiding the line of barrage balloons beside them.

This meant he actually passed over the battleship anchorage on his way towards the inner harbour. When the Swordfish reached the eastern part of the city he banked slightly, to fly around the northern rim of the Mar Piccolo while he peered through the darkness, looking for targets. He also dropped his altitude to 1,500 feet. Like the other bomber pilots Forde found the heavy cruisers obscured by smoke and darkness, but he spotted the row of ships moored stern-first to the quayside. He banked round to line himself up for an east-to-west run along the line of ships, which to him resembled sardines in a can. He dropped his six bombs at a cluster of likely targets – two larger ships (possibly light cruisers) and a destroyer. The first bombs splashed harmlessly into the harbour, and the rest might have hit something, but Forde and Mardel-Ferreira could not be sure. In fact, they could not even tell if all the bombs had released properly. So, Forde decided to go round again.

This was an act of immense courage, as the anti-aircraft fire was extremely heavy. However, Forde calmly circled clockwise around the Mar Piccolo, and made a second attack run. The two cruisers opened up a fearsome fire, but amazingly L4H emerged without a scratch. Once Forde was happy his bombs had been expended he wheeled away towards the north-west, and crossed over the coast five miles to the north of Taranto. As he flew away he could see a huge fire raging over the seaplane base bombed by Sarra and Barker.

The last of the four bombers was E5Q, crewed by Murray and Paine. They followed

Despite its antiquated design and slow speed the Fairey Swordfish was a versatile aircraft which was so useful that it remained in service throughout the war. The Mark I version used at Taranto was constructed using fabric stretched over a wooden frame, which meant the air frame could absorb a lot of damage without unduly affecting the aircraft's performance.

A Swordfish Mark II being readied for take-off on board an Illustrious-class aircraft carrier. Although originally designed as a TSR – a combined torpedo-bomber, gunnery spotter and reconnaissance plane – the Swordfish could also be adapted to carry other ordnance, including mines, bombs and rockets.

FROM LEFT TO RIGHT:
Captain Ollie Patch RM (Pilot, E5A), Lt. Michael 'Tiffy' Torrens-Spence (Pilot, L5C), Lt. Norman 'Blood' Scarlett (Observer, L4A), Lt. Richard Janvrin (Observer, L4P).

behind L4H as it flew above and along the line of flares and, like the others, on reaching the inner harbour they discovered they could not see the heavy cruisers at their moorings. So, like Forde and Mardel-Ferreira, they decided to run along the row of ships backing on to the quayside of the dockyard. They circled round to line up on their target, and flew along the row from east to west. They aimed for a destroyer – the *Libeccio* – but only one of their six bombs hit the target. Even then it failed to explode.

All in all the bombing runs had been disappointing. The principal targets – the three heavy cruisers *Trento*, *Trieste* and *Bolzano* – had not been spotted, their captains having wisely decided to avoid firing their guns and to rely on the darkness for cover. So, the bombs had been dropped over lesser targets, and even then, apart from those dropped over the seaplane base, they achieved nothing. After completing his bombing run Murray banked to port, and flew back over the eastern portion of the town, heading eastwards towards the Italian heel, and the open sea beyond. By contrast the torpedoes had caused immense damage and, as the noise of engines disappeared, the crews of the *Littorio* and *Conti di Cavour* were busy trying to save their ships. The time was now 11.35pm. The whole attack had lasted no more than 23 minutes from start to finish. However, the anti-aircraft guns around the harbour continued to blaze away for another ten minutes, until it was apparent that the attack was over.

FROM LEFT TO RIGHT:
S/ Lt. Peter 'Jonah' Jones (Observer, L5H), Lt. Edward Clifford (Pilot, L5F), Lt. Ronald Bailey (Observer, L4K), S/Lt. Buscall (Observer, L4M).

THE SECOND WAVE

Second wave (Lt. Cdr. Hale)

Swordfish (ordnance carried)	Squadron	Pilot	Observer	Note
L5A (torpedo)	819	Lt. Cdr. J. D. Hale	Lt. G. A. Carline	
L5H (torpedo)	819	Lt. C. Lea	S/Lt. P. D. Jones	
L5K (torpedo)	819	Lt. F. Torrens-Spence	Lt. A. Sutton	
E4H (torpedo)	813	Lt. G. Bayley	Lt. H. Slaughter	Shot down, crew killed
E5H (torpedo)	824	Lt. J. Wellham	Lt. P. Humphreys	
E5B (16 flares, 4 bombs)	819	Lt. R. Hamilton	S/Lt. J. Weekes	
L4F (16 flares, 4 bombs)	815	Lt. R. Skelton	S/Lt. E. A. Perkins	
L5F (6 bombs)	819	Lt. E. W. Clifford	Lt. G. R. Going	Take-off aborted
L5Q (6 bombs)	819	Lt. A. Morford	S/Lt. M. Greene	Mission aborted

Note: the prefix 'E' designated an aircraft from Eagle, 'L' from Illustrious.

While the first wave was still on its way to Taranto, Captain Boyd reduced speed to 17 knots, and turned *Illustrious* in a large 30-mile-diameter circle, designed to bring the carrier back to Point 'X for X-Ray' at the time designated for the launch of the second wave. By 9.00pm the Swordfish had been brought up from the hangar, and arrayed on the flight deck. Their crews appeared and were strapped in. They then made their final checks and preparations, while the minutes ticked by until the launch time. Most if not all of the 18 young men sitting in the planes must have wondered what their chances of survival might be. Unlike the men of the first wave, there would be no element of surprise, and they knew they would be flying into a hornet's nest of enemy fire. Lieutenant Lea remembered commenting, 'Let's hope the Eyeties run out of ammunition before we get there!'

At 9.15pm the aircraft carrier reached the launch point, and Captain Boyd turned it into the wind, increasing speed as he did so. With the wind sweeping the flight deck the crews strained to see the launch signal. Then at 9.20pm precisely, they saw the green flashing light from the bridge – Commander Robertson's signal to launch. One by one the pilots revved their engines, the chocks were removed and they began their take-off. The lead plane was flown by the wave leader, Lieutenant Commander 'Ginger' Hale in Swordfish L5A. As he and his observer Lieutenant Carline took off, the next plane was already speeding forward. As before, the aim was to launch the planes at ten-second intervals. The first seven Swordfish roared into the air successfully, but the eighth aircraft got into difficulties. L5F, crewed by Clifford and Going began moving forward, but then the chocks were removed from the ninth plane at its rear – L5Q, crewed by Morford and Greene.

The last Swordfish began to roll forward too, and seconds later the two aircraft collided with each other. Their biplane wings locked together, and they became entangled. Both pilots cut their engines while the flight deck crew raced to disentangle the two planes. Once the aircraft were separated it was discovered that the fabric of L5F had been damaged, both on the main fuselage and on the wing. It would not be flying that evening. However, L5Q was undamaged. When Captain Boyd and Commander Robertson were updated, they decided that Morford and Greene should take off as planned. By contrast, L5F would be taken back to the hangar for repairs – a crushing blow for Clifford and Going. Meanwhile the other six Swordfish had formed

up around the wave leader in L5A, five miles ahead of the carrier. Hale waited to see what was happening to his last two aircraft. Finally, at 9.45pm, L5Q raced up to join them, and a signal lamp from Robertson on *Illustrious* gave the order 'Carry On'. That was it – the second wave was on its way.

Twenty minutes later another aircraft had to pull out. Morford and Greene, flying L5Q, the last remaining bomber, suddenly felt a jolt. It was one of the straps holding their long-range fuel tank in place. On the torpedo-carrying planes, these were strapped above the after cockpit, but on the bomb-carrying planes, or on those carrying both bombs and parachute flares, the tank was strapped below the fuselage. Obviously it had been damaged in the collision, and nobody had noticed – until now. Seconds later the second metal strap gave way, and the tank fell into the sea. The engine cut out, and the plane started losing altitude fast, but Morford quickly switched the fuel to the main tank, and nursed the engine back into life, after a hair-raising free-fall drop of 1,000 feet. Still, they now had no option but to turn back, as they did not have enough fuel for the return trip to Taranto. So, they turned around, and flew back to *Illustrious*. As they approached, a barrage of anti-aircraft fire greeted them, until Greene fired a recognition signal, and they were able to land safely. That meant Hale's wave now consisted of just seven planes. He watched L5Q stall, but was unable to help. The remaining Swordfish continued on their way.

To make up for lost time, Hale increased speed, to bring them over their target at the assigned time. The second wave missed the thick cloud encountered by Williamson's first wave, but there were still patchy clouds to fly through, and the night seemed to be pitch black. However, at 10.50pm the sky cleared slightly, and Hale led the other seven aircraft up to their approach height of 8,000 feet. Twenty-five minutes later, at 11.10pm, they spotted their objective, about 60 miles in front of them. Taranto was

illuminated by what looked like a large green cone of tracer, interspersed with flak bursts. It was a sobering sight, particularly as they knew that the first wave was still carrying out its attack somewhere in the midst of all that anti-aircraft fire. Of course, the Italian listening posts had also detected the engines of this second wave, and so many of the gunners kept firing. Carline, Hale's observer, confirmed their location after spotting the lighthouse on Punto Santa Maria di Luca 15 nautical miles away, on the eastern side of the Gulf of Taranto.

The cockpit of a Fairey Swordfish was basic compared with that of other wartime aircraft of a comparable size, but pilots found the aircraft a joy to fly, because of its manoeuvrability and ruggedness. Communication with the observer was carried out by means of a voice pipe rather than an internal radio.

They were on track. Sutton, the observer in L5C, even managed to pick up Italian opera on his radio, as they approached their target.

At 11.50pm Hale turned towards the north-east, to begin his approach to the anchorage. The seven aircraft were still flying at 8,000 feet. Five minutes later Hale's observer Carline flashed 'G' for 'go' on his torch, the signal that detached the two flare-dropping teams. These were Hamilton and Weeks in E5B L5B and Skelton and Perkins in L4F. They broke off and made their way towards the eastern side of the Mar Grande. The gunfire had slackened during the previous 20 minutes, since the First Wave had flown out of range, but there was still a prodigious amount of anti-aircraft fire over the harbour. The other five planes circled around outside the harbour as the flare droppers made their approach. As the two Swordfish appeared over the south-eastern side of the anchorage the volume of fire increased again, but the planes remained unscathed. Hamilton and Weekes flew in at 5,000 feet, and dropped their 16 flares in a line, roughly where the flares had been dropped during the first attack. Then Skelton and Perkins followed up behind them, dropping eight more. That meant that once again the battleships in the Mar Grande were now perfectly visible. It was now a little after 12.10am.

A depiction of the attack by artist Lawrence Bagley in 1968, showing one Swordfish climbing after releasing its torpedo, while the observer in another aircraft watches. The *Vittorio Veneto* is shown on the right, the *Littorio* on the left, and the *Giulio Cesare* in the background. (PRC Archive)

Hale led the remaining five Swordfish – all carrying torpedoes – towards the northern side of the Mar Grande, skirting the island of San Pietro and the submerged breakwater before crossing over the mainland near Punto Rondella. In fact he doubled back over the sea, before heading towards the harbour again, to confuse both the Italian gunners and their listening systems. Hale and his crews had considered their best approach, and decided to attack the battlefield anchorage from the north-west. The idea was to avoid the barrage balloons

The battleship *Caio Duilio* photographed on the day following the attack. Its upper deck was almost completely submerged, and was abandoned when its crew members found themselves unable to save their ship.

This British reconnaissance photograph taken on the afternoon of 12 November shows the battleship *Littorio*, with its forecastle under water, surrounded by a cluster of smaller vessels, including a submarine, the generator of which was powering the battleship, and a tanker, the crew of which were removing the battleship's fuel.

→ Tugs

← Submarine

← Naval Auxiliary

Tanker ↗

lining the Diga di Taratona, even though that meant flying closer to the bulk of the anti-aircraft batteries on the mainland and running any gauntlet of fire from the cruisers and destroyers lying in the outer anchorage. As soon as they appeared, the anti-aircraft fire seemed to be drawn in their direction.

Hale in L5A passed over Punto Rondella at 5,000 feet, and steadily dropped altitude as the plane approached its target. The anti-aircraft fire was so heavy that Hale had to weave his plane from side to side, trying to throw the gunners off their aim. As he flew, he noticed that the air was thick with the smell of cordite, from all the anti-aircraft fire. They also flew past a barge; they did not see in time to react that it was designed to carry a barrage balloon. Without realizing, they must have missed its cable in the dark. Then Hale spotted his target. L5A had skirted around the top of the line of barrage balloons protecting the western side of the battleship anchorage, and so was approaching the battleships from roughly the same angle as the second sub-flight of the first wave. Like them he spotted the *Littorio* ahead of him, and lined up on it. He dropped his altitude a little more, until he was just 30 feet from the surface of the harbour. Hale and Carline dropped their torpedo at a range of 700 yards and, after checking it was running smoothly, Hale banked sharply to starboard, pulling back on the stick as he did so and passing across the bow of the *Littorio*. He then continued towards the outer harbour again and left the Mar Grande by flying over the southern submerged breakwater.

A little behind him, Bayley and Slaughter in E4H also crossed over the mainland before entering the anchorage, but unlike their wave leader they decided to fly around the bottom of the line of barrage balloons blocking their path. They dropped altitude as they raced over the destroyers in the outer portion of the anchorage, and then began their turn, in a course designed to take them around the south of the three heavy cruisers lying behind the barrage balloons. This would have put them in an ideal place to launch a torpedo attack on the *Andrea Doria* or the *Vittorio Veneto*, but suddenly their plane was hit. Nearby, Torrens-Spence in L5C saw the orange flash, and watched the plane spin out of control. Swordfish E4H fell into the harbour close to the southernmost of the barrage balloon rafts, between the heavy cruiser *Gorizia* and the destroyer

Gioberti. Both Bayley and Slaughter were killed. Although nobody can be sure, it seems likely that the anti-aircraft guns of one of these two warships were responsible for bringing down the Swordfish – the second aircraft lost in the raid.

Lea and Jones in Swordfish L5H crossed the coast a little behind Hale's L5A, and astern of Bayley and Slaughter's plane. Any attempt at keeping formation was abandoned because of the intensity of the flak. Lea decided to keep well to the north of the barrage balloons, and so he flew over the northern shore of the anchorage, before curving round towards the Italian battleships. He was still too high to launch his torpedo, so he calmly put his aircraft into a tight turn to starboard, pushing back on the stick as he turned. The plane spiralled down towards the harbour, and part of the way through the turn he saw the *Caio Diulio* in front of him, beam on.

He levelled out at 20 feet and made his torpedo run, launching his torpedo 800 yards away from his target. Lea immediately turned away, but Jones watched as the torpedo ran straight towards the battleship. It struck the *Caio Diulio* on its starboard side, just beneath 'B' turret. The explosion sent up a fountain of water, but by then Lea and Jones were already making their escape, banking tight to starboard and climbing, as they flew over the Italian cruisers lying beyond the battleship anchorage. They were so low they almost struck the mast of an anchored fishing boat. Lea weaved past the heavy cruisers *Fiume* and *Zara*, and then headed towards the island of San Pietro. As they passed over one of the cruisers at just 30 feet, Lee recalled that the shockwaves from its anti-aircraft guns jerked him in his seat. It seemed as if every gun in the harbour was firing directly at them, but they emerged unscathed, and reached the safety of the open sea. Lea turned and looked back, and was mesmerized by a glow behind him. It was only when it grew larger that he realized it was a 'flaming onion' of flak. He twisted the plane out of the way, and flew on into the darkness.

Torrens-Spence and Sutton in L5C flew directly over Punto Rondella to reach the Mar Grande, and then dived steeply, trying to keep parallel to the northern shore of the anchorage until they saw the canal leading to the Mar Piccolo. That would be Torrens-Spence's marker, telling him when to begin his turn towards the battleships. Suddenly he saw E4H approaching fast from the left – almost on a collision course. He turned to avoid Bailey and Slaughter's plane, then found

he had flown through the barrage balloon cables, and was now just to the north of the heavy cruiser anchorage. Then he saw the canal to his left. The anti-aircraft fire was ferocious. As the pilot said later, 'All the enemy close-range weapons had opened fire. We could see multiple batteries by the entrance to the inner harbour pouring stuff out right next to our dropping position – tracer, and incendiaries, and horrible things called flaming onions'. Somehow Torrens-Spence ignored the tracer, and made his turn to starboard. It was then that he spotted the *Littorio*. The angle of

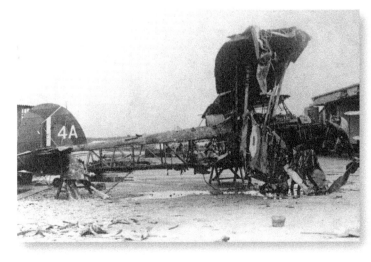

The remains of L4A, the Fairey Swordfish crewed by Lieutenant Commander Williamson and Lieutenant Scarlett, which crashed into the harbour after attacking the *Conti di Cavour*. Both Williamson and Scarlett survived the crash, but after being rescued they were taken prisoner.

3 2

BRITISH AIRCRAFT
1. L5A (torpedo), Hale & Carline
2. L5H (torpedo), Lea & Jones
3. L5K (torpedo), Torrens-Spence & Sutton
4. E4H (torpedo), Bayley & Slaughter
5. E5H (torpedo), Wellham & Humphreys
6. E5B (flares & bombs), Hamilton & Weekes
7. L4F (flares & bombs), Skelton & Perkins
8. L5F (bombs), Clifford & Going

SUBMERGED
BREAKWATER

ISLA SAN PIETRO

A A
(ANTI-AIRCRAFT
BATTERIES)

SUBMERGED
BREAKWATER

ISOLETTO
SAN PAOLO

DIGA
SAN VI

C. SAN VITO

EVENTS

1. 12.10am: the flare-dropping aircraft E5B (Hamilton & Weekes) and L4F (Skelton & Perkins) drop their flares on the eastern side of the Mar Grande, to illuminate the battleships for the approaching torpedo bombers.

2. 12.12am: Swordfish L5A (Hale & Carline) approaches the battleship anchorage by flying over the western suburbs of Taranto. Hale selects the *Littorio* as his target, but the torpedo narrowly misses the battleship.

3. 12.13am: Bayley & Slaughter in Swordfish E4H try to work their way round the southern end of the line of barrage balloons screening the western approach to the battleship and cruiser anchorages, but the aircraft receives a direct hit from an anti-aircraft shell, and it crashes into the harbour near the cruiser *Gorizia*. Both crew members are killed.

4. 12.14am: approaching the battleship anchorage some way behind the wing leader, L5H (Lea & Jones) finds itself in an ideal position from which to attack the *Caio Duilio*. Lea launches his torpedo and turns away, skimming over the top of a fishing boat as he banks. His torpedo strikes the starboard side of the Italian battleship, which immediately begins to settle.

5. 12.16am: Swordfish L5K (Torrens-Spence & Sutton) is the last of the four aircraft to approach the battleship anchorage from the same direction. They see Bayley & Slaughter's plane go down, but press on, flying through the line of barrage balloons and the cruiser anchorage to reach a firing position off the starboard bow of the *Littorio*. Their torpedo strikes the battleship, which immediately begins to list heavily.

6. 12.16am: the two flare-dropping aircraft E5B and L4F circle around to the east and launch a bombing attack on the oil storage depot, which was already attacked by the flare droppers of the first wave.

7. 12.16am: the final torpedo-armed Swordfish in the wave is E5H (Wellham & Humphreys). Rather than get in the way of the others, Wellham circles around the eastern side of the battleship anchorage.

8. 12.20am: E5H drops down to make its attack from the south-east. The aircraft is damaged during its run in, but Wellham circles around and fires his torpedo at the *Vittorio Veneto*. Although the torpedo misses, the aircraft is fortunate enough to remain in the air, despite receiving further damage before it can escape.

9. 12.25am: having taken off 15 minutes behind the other aircraft in the wave because of damage suffered on the flight deck, L5F (Clifford & Going) arrive over Taranto as the last of the torpedo-armed planes depart. After circling around the port to the west, Clifford carries out a bombing run on the heavy cruiser *Trento*, moored in the Mar Piccolo. Although one bomb hits the vessel, it fails to explode. By 12.35am L5F has flown out of range of the anti-aircraft defences of the port.

THE ATTACK ON TARANTO – THE SECOND WAVE, 12.10–12.35AM, 12 NOVEMBER 1940

The second wave of Swordfish appears over Taranto an hour after the first wave, and just over half an hour after the earlier attack has ended. It comprises fewer planes than the first wave – just seven aircraft, with an eighth aircraft attacking 20 minutes after the rest of the wave. This second wave is led by Lt. Cdr. Hale, who orders his aircraft to begin their approach shortly before midnight.

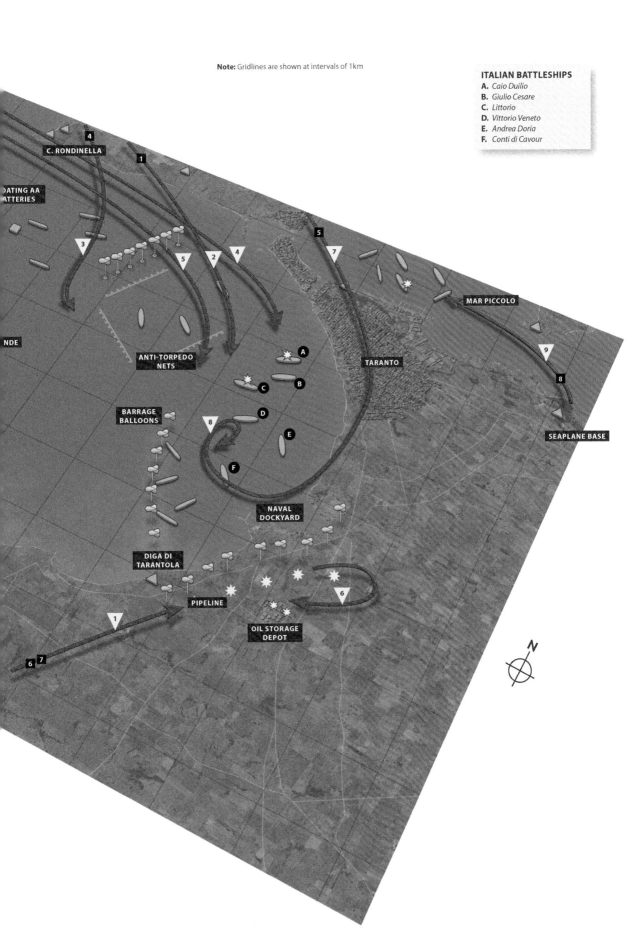

Note: Gridlines are shown at intervals of 1km

ITALIAN BATTLESHIPS
A. *Caio Duilio*
B. *Giulio Cesare*
C. *Littorio*
D. *Vittorio Veneto*
E. *Andrea Doria*
F. *Conti di Cavour*

C. RONDINELLA

OATING AA
ATTERIES

MAR PICCOLO

NDE

ANTI-TORPEDO
NETS

TARANTO

A

C

B

BARRAGE
BALLOONS

D

E

SEAPLANE BASE

F

NAVAL
DOCKYARD

DIGA DI
TARANTOLA

PIPELINE

OIL STORAGE
DEPOT

N

attack was less than perfect, but he realized that the planes could be hit at any second, and so he decided to launch his torpedo.

At first it did not release. Torrens-Spence tried again, and this time the mechanism worked. The torpedo was dropped 700 yards from the *Littorio*, off its starboard bow. They were about 20 feet from the harbour – lower probably, as at one point their wheels were skimming the surface of the water. The torpedo's angle of attack was about 45°, making the battleship a harder target, and it duly missed, burying itself in the mud of the harbour somewhere to the south-east of the damaged battleship. As L5C climbed away to the right Torrens-Spence spotted two floating gun batteries ahead of him, and both were firing directly at him – so close both he and Sutton could feel the heat from their fire. *Littorio* was also firing. As Torrens-Spence recalled, 'The flash of her close range weapons stabbed at us, as first one and then another along her length opened up.' He continued, 'We were in the centre of an incredible mass of crossfire from the cruisers and battleships and shore batteries.' They were even fired on from gunboats guarding the harbour entrance, as they flew past the southern breakwater. Amazingly, they emerged from the battleship anchorage with only one bullet hole in the fuselage of their plane.

That left one last torpedo plane, E5H, crewed by Wellham and Humphreys. They had passed over the coast a little to the north of Hale, and actually flew over the Mar Piccolo, losing altitude as they went, before passing over the easternmost portion of the city. It was close enough to make out individual walls, streets, buildings and gardens. Wellham looped around the eastern side of the Mar Grande, before approaching the battleship anchorage from the east. The whole area was lit by gun flashes and ribbons of tracer. Strangely though, the two crewmen noticed that none of this fire seemed to be directed at them. It was almost as if they were approaching their target without being seen. That, though, was about to change.

This unique line of approach meant that Wellham avoided all of the barrage balloons, but on passing them the Swordfish attracted an undue proportion of defensive fire from the anti-aircraft batteries protecting Taranto itself. As he turned towards the ships, tracer rounds ripped through his

The forward superstructure of the battleship *Caio Duilio*, pictured after the attack. It was hit by one torpedo on its starboard side, which blew a hole below its waterline beneath its forward turrets. It was beached in shallow water, to prevent it from sinking completely.

aileron. The plane seemed to stagger in mid-air, and Wellham had to fight hard to regain control of his aircraft as it side-slipped towards the water. It was worth it – when E5H emerged over the Mar Grande near the small dockyard there, Wellham found he had a rich choice of targets. Four battleships lay within reach of his torpedo. He circled around, flying within 30 feet of the water, and selected the *Vittorio Veneto*. Wellham and Humphreys launched their torpedo 500 yards from the battleship, then banked sharply to make their escape.

The torpedo ran past the battleship, but went on to strike the already damaged *Conti di Cavour*, which lay behind it. The Italian gunners followed the plane as it tried to bank away, and tracer chased them across the harbour. As they flew towards the safety of the breakwater a 40mm pom-pom round struck their lower port wing and exploded. It punched a large hole in the fabric, and broke several of its wooden ribs, but once again Wellham fought to keep control of his aircraft, and flew on, heading out of the Mar Grande by way of the submerged breakwater, just north of San Pietro Island. Fabric was flapping from the wing, and the aileron controls did not respond properly, but they were still airborne, and flying home.

After dropping their flares, Hamilton and Weekes in E5B and Skelton and Perkins in L4F both circled to the right, dropped altitude, and then flew parallel to the line of flares, half a mile farther inland, until they reached the Italian Navy's oil storage depot. It was easily visible, thanks to the bombs dropped there by the flare-dropping planes of the first wave. The two planes approached the target, having split up to attack it from different angles and in succession. They released their bombs over the depot at an altitude of about 2,500 feet. Weekes noted that E5B had scored hits of some kind, as flames shot skyward, but Perkins was convinced his plane had missed. Then the two pilots banked away, and headed towards the coast well to the south of Taranto. As they departed, the observers also had a grandstand view of the torpedo planes as they carried out their attacks. The departure of Wellham and Humphreys should have brought the second wave – indeed the whole strike – to an end. However, there was one last curtain call, made by a plane that was not expected to be there.

After being damaged on the flight deck, Swordfish L5F was wheeled to the lift, and taken down to the armoured hangar. There, Clifford and Going watched impatiently as a team of riggers raced to repair the tears in the fabric of the plane. Incredibly, this work was completed in just 15 minutes, and while Clifford supervised the repairs, Going pleaded with Commander Robertson and then Captain Boyd to let them fly after all. As Going pleaded his case, Clifford made sure that L5F was taken back to the flight deck and ranged on deck. Finally, 24 minutes after the other aircraft had taken off, Boyd gave his approval. Robertson's green light flashed, and Swordfish L5F took to the air, and then raced to follow the rest of the wave. It was a brave thing to do. They knew they had little chance of catching up with Hale, which meant that when it came time to launch their attack, they would be all on their own. That meant every Italian gun in Taranto would be firing at them.

Like the rest of the wave, Clifford and Going were guided to their target by the pyramid of anti-aircraft fire over Taranto. Going later said of the spectacle, 'It was the biggest firework display we had ever seen, and we were awestruck by it.' Clifford had made better time than the other planes ahead of him, but he still began his approach to the harbour after the other planes had departed. The anti-aircraft fire was beginning to die away again as they made landfall on the eastern side of the

The bows of the *Caio Duilio*, with the upper decks awash. Dramatic though this damage first appeared, the battleship was refloated within two months of the attack, and was back in service the following May.

ATTACK OF THE SECOND WAVE, SEEN FROM THE BATTLESHIP *LITTORIO* (PP. 78–79)

The second wave of Swordfish begins its attack shortly after midnight on 12 November. As before, flares are dropped beyond the south-east corner of the Mar Grande, which are meant to silhouette the Italian battleships, and make them easier to see for the attackers. In this wave there are only five torpedo-armed planes, one of which, E4H, is shot down during its approach to the battleship anchorage, and both of its crew are killed. Three of the remaining Swordfish make their approach runs from the north-west, and so they approach the anchorage from its northern side. The fifth torpedo-armed aircraft circles around the Mar Grande, and attacks the *Littorio* from the south. As during the first wave's attack, the shore-based anti-aircraft batteries lay a heavy flak barrage above the harbour **(1)**, which looks spectacular, but is no immediate threat to the attacking planes, as they are flying well below it. However, the warships in the Mar Grande all fire their smaller-calibre weapons at the attacking planes, and despite orders they fire some of their larger weapons as well. In this plate Italian seamen are shown manning the anti-aircraft guns on the starboard battery deck of the battleship *Littorio*. It is situated between the bridge superstructure and the forward funnel. On the right **(2)** are twin-barrelled 20mm close-range weapons, which are shown firing at Swordfish L5A **(3)**, which has just released its torpedo and is banking hard to starboard, to avoid flying into the battleship's bridge. In the foreground **(4)** are larger twin-barrelled 37mm anti-aircraft guns, which are also engaging the same target. Swordfish L5A is crewed by the second strike leader Lt. Cdr Hale (pilot) and Lt. Carline (observer). Hale releases his torpedo at a range of around 700 yards, and a height of 30 feet. Hale has to climb as well as bank to avoid the battleship, and flies over its bow before reaching the relative safety of the outer harbour. In the background Swordfish L5H crewed by Lt. Lea and Sub. Lt. Jones has just launched a torpedo that has struck the starboard side of the battleship *Caio Duilio* **(5)**. Behind Hale and Carline, Swordfish L5C, crewed by lieutenants Torrens-Spence and Sutton, is beginning its own torpedo run against the starboard beam of the *Littorio*.

Mar Grande. He flew to the east of the line of flares, the last of which were now falling to earth. Unlike the other planes of the wave, L5F was exclusively armed with bombs – six of them. Clifford's objectives were the ships in the Mar Piccolo. He circled around to the eastern side of the inner harbour, looking for a suitable target. Unlike the bombers of the first flight, he spotted the cluster of Italian heavy cruisers, illuminated by the glow from the seaplane base.

The cruisers lay just to the north of the quayside, with its line of smaller warships berthed stern on to it. Clifford dropped altitude from 2,500 to just 500 feet, and lined up on the nearest of the cruisers – the *Trento*. It was lying stern on to him, which made it slightly harder to hit, but increased the chances of hitting with more than one bomb if he was on target. Close to it lay its sister ship, the *Trieste*. Lines of tracer rose up from the dockyard and from several of the ships. Clifford and Going made

The quayside of the naval dockyard in the Mar Piccolo, pictured on the day following the attack. None of the ships here suffered any significant damage, although the photograph reveals a considerable amount of oil on the surface of the harbour. When a bomb pierced the side of the heavy cruiser *Trento*, a forward oil tank was ruptured.

their run, dropped their six bombs, and then turned away towards the north. Going did not see any explosions, so they thought they had missed. In fact one of the bombs had penetrated the hull of the *Trento*, but it failed to explode. The tracer chased them as they looped around the north of the Mar Piccolo, and then flew east then south, crossing the coast five miles below the port.

Going glanced back. He remembered seeing ships burning and the sheen of oil in the water of the Mar Grande; flames were shooting up the side of one of the battleships, and columns of smoke hung over the harbour. It looked as if the raid had gone well. The time was approximately 12.35am. As this last Swordfish departed, the anti-aircraft fire over Taranto slowly died away, as the listening stations reported the raiders had all flown out of range. It was far from quiet though – in the battleship anchorage there was still feverish activity, as the *Littorio*, *Conti di Cavour* and *Caio Duilio* settled onto the bottom of the harbour, and fire teams struggled to extinguish the flames, both on the battleships and in the two main targets on land – the seaplane base and the fuel depot. The men of the Italian Navy had a busy night ahead of them.

RETURN TO *ILLUSTRIOUS*

When the second wave took off from *Illustrious*, Captain Boyd turned the ship back onto its regular course, but then circled round to steam back into the wind, to allow Swordfish L5F to take off and chase after the other aircraft. Once Clifford and Going were airborne, the aircraft carrier reduced speed, and headed on a south-south-easterly course, which brought it slightly closer to the Greek Ionian Island of Cephalonia. At 11.15pm, at the same moment as Williamson's first wave was carrying out its attack, the carrier and its escorts reversed course, then altered slightly to starboard. The carrier was heading towards its next rendezvous position, 'Point Y for Yorker'. This was 25 miles due east of 'Point X for X-Ray', and 20 miles west of Kabbo Point on Cephalonia.

The battleship *Littorio* was hit by three torpedoes – two in the bow and one in the stern. The latter did little damage, save to the battleship's rudder, but the first two hits caused the battleship to sink by the bow. This photograph taken a few days after the attack shows the extent of the damage.

The aim was to be there by 1.00am on 12 November – roughly when the first Swordfish of the first strike were expected to return – if any of them survived. It was approximately 185 nautical miles from Taranto – a little over two hours' flying time.

When the returning planes got within 50 nautical miles of *Illustrious* they would pick up the ship's transponder signal, which would vector them towards the aircraft. The carrier's proximity to Cephalonia would also help the airmen find their way home. Radio silence was still being strictly enforced so, apart from the terse 'Attack completed' from the flight leaders, Lyster, Boyd, Robertson and the others on board *Illustrious* had no idea when the Swordfish would return. They were also expecting the worst. Boyd expected most of the planes would return, but thought the raiders would suffer heavy casualties. Robertson was a little more pessimistic, given the strong defences of the anchorage, and expected that planes managing to return might be heavily damaged. The first warning of their return would come by way of the ship's air warning radar, which in theory could detect aircraft at a range of approximately 40–60 nautical miles. Until then, there was nothing to do but wait.

At 1.00am *Illustrious* reached Point Y, and turned into the wind. Boyd also increased speed to 21 knots, to help increase the wind over the flight deck prior to landing. At 1.12am the radar team spotted a blip on its screen, 40 miles to the north-west. Other blips then appeared. The bridge was informed, and everyone who could, from rear admiral to flight deck crew, peered out into the darkness, over the port bow. Fire and crash teams stood ready to deal with any emergency, and the flight deck landing lights were switched on. The first aircraft home was L4C, crewed by Sparke and Neale. After Neale flashed their recognition signal, Sparke made his approach from astern of the carrier, and made a perfect landing. The time was approximately 1.40am. The other aircraft of the flight formed a circuit, and began landing at 30-second intervals. When it touched down, each Swordfish had its momentum checked by an arrester hook. Halfway up the flight deck was a net crash barrier, which was raised for each landing, then lowered when it was not required. One by one each Swordfish was rolled forward out of the way, to allow the next aircraft to land.

This slick operation continued, as Lyster, Boyd and Robertson watched from the bridge. The radar team had reported that they had spotted 11 aircraft, so they knew one aircraft was missing. Was it just lagging behind, or had it been shot down? It was only when all the Swordfish had landed that they realized the missing aircraft belonged to the wave leader, Lieutenant Commander Williamson. All the other planes landed safely, although Kemp, piloting L4K, rolled forward too quickly when his arrester hook was released, and his Swordfish crashed into the back of the aircraft in front of him.

Commander Robertson was a stickler for correct flight deck procedures, and normally he would have summoned the pilot and delivered a severe dressing down. On this occasion he decided to let the matter slide. As the crews clambered out of their aircraft they were greeted by grinning flight deck staff, and had to fight their way past the well-wishers to reach the Air Intelligence Office for their debriefing.

There they told Commander Beale about their experiences, as their reports were filed. From this Beale and the ship's intelligence section could get an idea of how well Taranto had been defended, and what damage had been inflicted. Nobody had seen Williamson and Scarlett go down, as everyone had been too busy carrying out his own attack. However, it was clear that several torpedo hits had been scored –

primarily on the *Littorio* – while other battleships might have been damaged as well. This vital task over, the crew trooped down to the wardroom, where the bar had been thrown open, despite the hour, and a big banner put up saying 'Welcome Home'. There was even a nocturnal meal of bacon and eggs, and a cake in the shape of a Swordfish, with pink icing. Then, at 1.35am, the first aircraft of the second wave appeared on the ship's radar screen. Celebrations were put on hold, as everyone who could went on deck to watch Hale and his companions come in to land.

The first to appear were Hale and Carline in L5A and Skelton and Perkins in L4F, who landed shortly after 2.00am. Wellham and Humphreys were next, with fabric hanging off their wing. Then, between 2.15am and 2.30am, L5C, E5B and L5H made their approach, and landed safely. That left two planes – the late starters Clifford and Going in L5F, and E4H, crewed by Bayley and Slaughter. Radar showed just one blip approaching, meaning one aircraft from the wave was missing. Finally, at 2.50am, Swordfish L5F landed back on board the carrier, to the cheers of everyone watching from the flight deck. It was the last of the raiders to return. In the debriefing by Commander Beale, it was confirmed that one plane had been shot down – Torrens-Spence and Sutton had seen the orange flash when it was hit. This confirmed that Bailey and Slaughter had been shot down.

Out of the 20 Swordfish that had taken part in the raid, two had been lost over Taranto. Despite the more pessimistic casualty rates most had imagined, this was exactly 10 per cent – the same figure Commander Willoughby of *Glorious* had estimated when the plan for the raid was presented to Admiral Pound just over two years before. Hale made his report to Captain Boyd. When asked how the attack had gone, Hale replied, 'Oh, all right, Sir.' When asked if he thought it had been a success, he expanded on this, saying, 'I think it might have been, Sir.' Boyd then asked him if there had been much flak. Hale's answer was, 'Quite a bit, Sir.' The understatement was what everyone expected from such a cool and imperturbable leader. Exasperated, Boyd sent the aircrews down to the wardroom, so the celebrations could begin anew.

In this British reconnaissance photograph the location of the stricken *Conti di Cavour* is marked by a large oil slick, while the undamaged *Vittorio Veneto* can be seen off its starboard beam. The *Conti di Cavour* was beached to prevent it from sinking completely, and abandoned by its crew. The 'Y' shaped structure at the top of the photograph is a refuelling jetty.

Battle of the Strait of Otranto, 12 November 1940

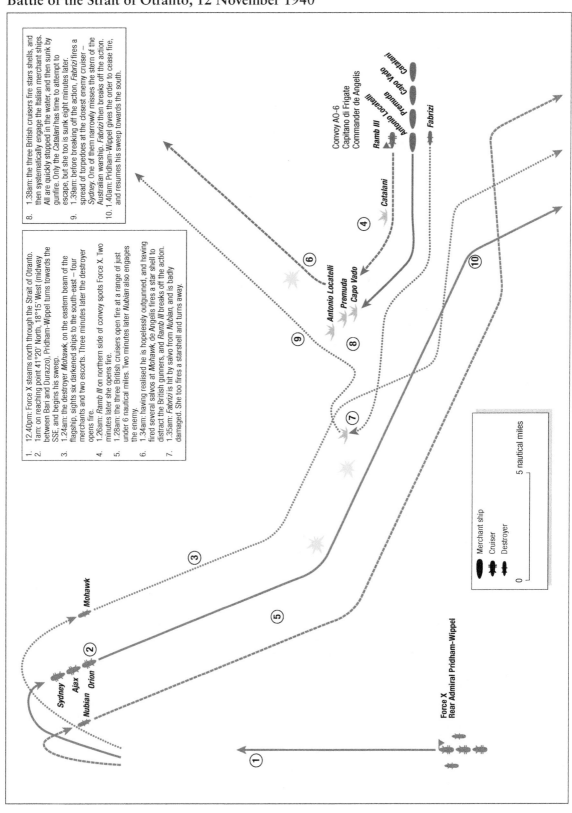

1. 12.40pm: Force X steams north through the Strait of Otranto.
2. 1am: on reaching point 41°20' North, 18°15' West (midway between Bari and Durazzo), Pridham-Wippel turns towards the SSE, and begins his sweep.
3. 1.24am: the destroyer *Mohawk*, on the eastern beam of the flagship, sights six darkened ships to the south-east – four merchants and two escorts. Three minutes later the destroyer opens fire.
4. 1.26am: *Ramb III* on northern side of convoy spots Force X. Two minutes later she opens fire.
5. 1.28am: the three British cruisers open fire at a range of just under 6 nautical miles. Two minutes later *Nubian* also engages the enemy.
6. 1.34am: having realised he is hopelessly outgunned, and having fired several salvos at *Mohawk*, de Angelis fires a star shell to distract the British gunners, and *Ramb III* breaks off the action.
7. 1.35am: *Fabrizi* is hit by salvo from *Nubian*, and is badly damaged. She too fires a starshell and turns away.

8. 1.38am: the three British cruisers fire stars shells, and then systematically engage the Italian merchant ships. All are quickly stopped in the water, and then sunk by gunfire. Only the *Catalani* has time to attempt to escape, but she too is sunk eight minutes later.
9. 1.39am: before breaking off the action, *Fabrizi* fires a spread of torpedoes at the closest enemy cruiser – *Sydney*. One of them narrowly misses the stern of the Australian warship. *Fabrizi* then breaks off the action.
10. 1.40am: Pridham-Wippel gives the order to cease fire, and resumes his sweep towards the south.

84

As they did, Commander Robertson and Commander Beale pored over the reports, trying to estimate the degree of damage the raid had caused. In truth they would not know properly until a reconnaissance Maryland could fly over Taranto the following morning.

All the indications, however, were that the raid had been a success. Lyster and Robertson then had a decision to make. If the Italian ships were damaged, but not put out of action, then they might have to send the aircrews back to Taranto the following night. This time though, the defenders would be ready, and casualties were bound to be greater than before. When the aircrews were told about this, one wag quipped, 'Good God – they only asked the Light Brigade to do it once!' In the end, the reconnaissance photos revealed that three Italian battleships had been sunk or beached, and would be unserviceable for some considerable time. That represented half of the Italian battleship force. Given that news, and his reluctance to risk his exhausted aircrews on a second mission, Lyster decided to break off the operation, and rejoin the rest of the Mediterranean Fleet.

In the Strait of Otranto, just after midnight on 12 November, Pridham-Wippell's Force X (*Orion*, *Ajax*, *Synes* and the destroyers *Mohawk* and *Nubian*) reached the main Italian convoy route between Bari and Durazzo (now Durrës in Albania), and began searching for the Italians. They had the advantage of radar, and at 1.00am they detected a small Italian convoy of four merchant ships, escorted by the auxiliary cruiser *Ramb III* and the torpedo boat *Fabrizi*. Twenty-seven minutes later the British ships opened fire. The Italian warships were hopelessly outnumbered and outgunned. After a brief gun duel both escorts broke away, *Fabrizi* having been badly damaged in the exchange. All four merchant ships were sunk. The British ships were unscathed, although a torpedo from *Fabrizi* had narrowly missed the *Sydney* during the climax of the fight. Force X then headed south to rejoin Admiral Cunningham.

While Operation *Judgement* had been taking place, Cunningham's Force A had been 100 nautical miles to the south, screening Convoy ME3, as well as covering both Pridham-Wippell's Force X and Lyster's carrier force. Both detached forces rejoined the fleet during the late morning of 12 November. As *Illustrious* came within range, a flag signal from Cunningham appeared on the masthead of *Warspite*. It read simply: '*Illustrious*: Manoeuvre well executed.' This was another understatement – Cunningham was delighted. Later that day, Cunningham sent a signal to the rest of the Mediterranean Fleet. It read: '*Illustrious*' aircraft carried out most successful raid on Taranto. Estimated that one Littorio and two Cavour torpedoed, and many fires started by bombs. All aircraft returned but two'. As Sir Winston Churchill pointed out in the House of Commons two days later, in the fight for control of the Mediterranean, the attack had dramatically tilted the odds in Britain's favour.

COUNTING THE COST

The first warning the defenders of Taranto had of the attack came from the listening stations on the coast. The air raid warning was sounded, and the anti-aircraft guns were manned and made ready. When the attack began, Ammiraglio di Squadra Campioni received a string of reports. They told him that the *Conti di Cavour* had been hit, and was taking on water. Then two torpedoes hit the *Littorio*. Other more garbled reports reached him, of damage to cruisers in the Mar Piccolo, and to both the seaplane base and the oil storage depot. The fires in both these shore facilities were soon put out. At the seaplane base the serious damage was limited to one hangar, where two aircraft were destroyed. At the fuel depot, initial reports of raging fires proved inaccurate, and only one secondary pipeline was damaged. It had seemed more serious at the time, because of the burning fuel. Similarly there was no significant damage to the warships in the Mar Piccolo.

During the second attack, the *Caio Duilio* was hit on its starboard side, while the *Littorio* was struck for the third time, also on its starboard side. Finally in the Mar Piccolo the decks of the heavy cruiser *Trento* and the destroyer *Libeccio* were both pierced by one bomb apiece, but both failed to explode before passing through the ships' hulls into the harbour. Therefore they caused no serious damage. However, three battleships were in serious difficulties, thanks to five torpedo hits – three caused by the first wave of attackers, and two by the second:

Torpedoes fired at Italian battleships

Battleship	First Wave	Second Wave	Total Fired	Hits
Littorio	2 (both hits)	3 (1 hit)	5	3
Vittorio Veneto	1	1	2	
Caio Duilio		1	1	1
Andrea Doria				
Giulio Cesare				
Conti di Cavour	3 (1 hit)		3	1

It was not until daylight that Campioni could gain a clear idea of the damage to his battleships. The night had been spent organizing salvage and repair parties, sending tugs and auxiliaries to tow two of the battleships to shallow waters, and dealing with the dead and wounded. Oil covered the surface of both the Mar Grande and the Mar Piccolo – the latter from a punctured oil tank in the *Trento*. For sailors and civilians alike the scene of devastation was heartbreaking. That morning the Italian radio claimed that only one battleship had been damaged, for the loss of six attacking aircraft, while three more were so badly damaged they crashed on their way home to Crete. Even after interviewing the two captured airmen – Williamson and Scarlett – the Italians still ruled out the possibility of a carrier-based attack, and assumed the British aircraft had flown from Crete. In fact, of the six battleships that comprised the core of the Italian battle fleet, three had been put out of action. One of these was damaged beyond repair. However Mussolini might describe it, it was a black day for the Italian Navy.

Littorio had been struck by three torpedoes. The first (inflicted by Kemp and Bailey in L4K) was in its starboard bow, where a 50ft by 32ft hole was blown in the Pugliese torpedo bulge just below 'B' turret, the blast penetrating the outer hull and inner torpedo bulkhead behind it. This led to heavy flooding, and the battleship began to list then settle by the bows. The second torpedo hit (caused by Swayne and Buscall in L4M) had hit *Littorio* in its starboard quarter, creating a 26ft by 5ft rip in its hull, just abreast of its tiller flat. This severely damaged the battleship's port rudder, and put its steering gear out of action. Here though, the flooding was relatively easily confined to just two of the ship's aftermost watertight compartments. During the second strike *Littorio* was hit by the third torpedo (delivered by Torrens-Spence and Sutton in L5C). It hit the battleship at the base of its Pugliese bulge on its starboard side, beneath 'A' turret, blowing a 40ft by 32ft hole in its side, which caused extensive flooding. The Pugliese system was designed to let the anti-torpedo bulge absorb the blast, thus preserving the hull behind it. The system did not work. This was the most serious hit of the three.

By morning *Littorio* was down by the bows, its foredeck under water as far as 'B' turret. A cluster of smaller vessels came to its aid – tow auxiliaries, a tanker, and even a submarine, whose generator provided the stricken battleship with the power needed to work its electric pumps. It is a testimony to the design of *Littorio* and to the skills of the Ansaldo shipyard in Genoa that it took so much punishment and survived. Incidentally, an unexploded torpedo was discovered lying beneath the battleship's stern, matching a dent in its starboard quarter. This suggested it was hit a fourth time, but the torpedo failed to detonate. Before it could be moved, this torpedo had to be defused and removed. It was not until 11 December – a month after the attack – that it could be moved into a dry dock. It remained there until the following March, when it was able to rejoin the fleet.

The *Conti di Cavour* was hit once, but the damage inflicted on this older battleship was more severe than that caused to the *Littorio*. It had been hit by the torpedo dropped by Williamson and Scarlett in L4A, seconds before their Swordfish was shot down. The battleship was struck on its port bow, immediately below 'A' turret, and because the 40ft by 30ft hole overlapped the edge of its armoured citadel, it also spanned more than one watertight compartment. The detonation blasted through two oil tanks located in the void behind its outer hull, and penetrated the inner hull behind them. The crew was fortunate that the blast did not penetrate as far as the forward magazines. These compartments flooded immediately, but not before the water had reached adjacent compartments. The ship lost electrical power, and began to go down by the bows. It was saved only by the skill of its captain, who called on support to move it and beached it in the shallows before it sank even farther. At 5.45am the *Conti di Cavour* was abandoned by its crew, and the following day (13 November) it was handed over to a salvage company from Trieste, which began the task of raising it. It was finally refloated in July 1941, after all its guns and sections of its armour had been removed. After further repairs to its hull it was moved to Trieste, where it remained for the duration of the war.

The last of the three battleship casualties was the *Caio Duilio*. During the second attack it was struck by a torpedo launched by Lea and James in L5H. The torpedo struck it low down on its starboard side, 30 feet below the waterline, beneath 'A' and 'B' turrets. Like on the *Conti di Cavour*, this hit

The Australian light cruiser HMAS *Sydney*, which formed part of Rear Admiral Pridham-Wippell's Force X, and which took part in the battle of the Strait of Otranto. Four months earlier, off Cape Spada in Crete, *Sydney* was responsible for the sinking of the Italian light cruiser *Bartolomeo Colleoni*.

was dangerously close to the ship's forward main magazines, but the torpedo explosion did not ignite the explosives in them, and thanks to the quick thinking of the crew the magazines were deliberately flooded to prevent any such disaster. The blast punctured its lower hull, ripping a 40ft by 26ft hole in its side. The battleship began settling by the bow. However, unlike the *Conti di Cavour*, its damage control parties managed to seal off the watertight compartments quickly enough to prevent the flooding from spreading aft through the ship. Shortly before dawn it was beached with the help of a nearby water tanker and two auxiliary tugs, to avoid any further risk of foundering. After being refloated the following January the *Caio Duilio* was taken to Genoa for repairs, and it rejoined the fleet in May 1941.

Even with the benefit of hindsight it is difficult to see what the Italians could have done to prevent the raiders from inflicting so much damage. Certainly more torpedo nets and barrage balloons would have made the task much harder for the Fleet Air Arm crews, but no such attack had ever been attempted before, so it was difficult for the defenders to gauge what was an appropriate level of defence for the fleet. While the port defenders were criticized for their failure to shoot down more aircraft, the same lack of exposure to this kind of attack made it hard to formulate an adequate plan to safeguard the fleet. For a start, the anti-aircraft barrage had been ferocious. No fewer than 1,430 12.5cm, 313 10.7cm and 6,854 8.8cm rounds had been expended by the shore batteries, as well as 931 40mm and 2,635 20mm rounds. A further 637 8mm machine-gun bullets had been fired. The trouble was, the fire plan quite rightly did not allow the guns to fire at too low a trajectory over the Mar Grande or Mar Piccolo, for fear of hitting friendly ships. Most of the time the torpedo-armed Swordfish were flying below the level of the barrage.

The warships in the anchorage were allowed to fire only lower-calibre weapons (40mm and below), as point defence weapons – in other words to defend their own ship. Again, orders precluded them from being fired at a low elevation in the crowded anchorage, unless the gunners enjoyed a field of fire unencumbered by other warships. From the testimony of the British aircrews it seems that at times these restrictions were ignored, as they encountered low-level fire while they flew between the Italian ships. In the circumstances it is surprising that the moored warships did not suffer damage or casualties from the guns of their neighbouring vessels. Given the scale of destruction the casualties suffered during the raid were surprisingly light. A total of 23 crew members had been killed on board the *Littorio*, as well as a further 16 on the *Conti di Cavour* and one on the *Caio Duilio*. If one of the torpedoes had hit a magazine – and two came perilously close – the death toll would have been considerably higher.

Rear Admiral Pridham-Wippell's flagship in November 1940 was the Leander-class light cruiser *Orion*, a sister ship of *Ajax*, which also took part in the night action in the Strait of Otranto. Pridham-Wippell's operation took place on the same evening as the Taranto raid.

AFTERMATH

On 13 November, when Sir Winston Churchill broke the news to the British House of Commons, he said:

> The Royal Navy has struck a crippling blow at the Italian Fleet. The total strength of the Italian battle fleet was six battleships, two of them of the 'Littorio' class, which have just been put into service and are, of course, among the most powerful vessels in the world, and four of the recently reconstructed 'Cavour' class. This fleet was, to be sure, considerably more powerful on paper than our Mediterranean Fleet, but it had consistently refused to accept battle.
>
> On the night of the 11–12 November, when the main units of the Italian Fleet were lying behind their shore defences in their naval base at Taranto, our aircraft of the Fleet Air Arm attacked them in their stronghold. Reports of our airmen have been confirmed by photographic reconnaissance. It is now established that one battleship of the Littorio class was badly down by the bows and that its forecastle is under water and it has a heavy list to starboard. One battleship of the 'Cavour' class has been beached, and its stern, up to and including the after turret, is under water. This ship is also heavily listed to starboard. It has not yet been possible to establish the fact with certainty, but it appears that a second battleship of the 'Cavour' class has also been severely damaged and beached.
>
> The Italian communiqué of 12 November, in admitting that one warship had been severely damaged, claimed that six of our aircraft had been shot down and three more probably. In fact, only two of our aircraft are missing, and it is noted that the enemy claimed that part of the crews had been taken prisoner.
>
> I felt it my duty to bring this glorious episode to the immediate notice of the House. As the result of a determined and highly successful attack, which reflects the greatest honour on the Fleet Air Arm, only three Italian battleships now remain effective. This result, while it affects decisively the balance of naval power in the Mediterranean, also carries with it reactions upon the naval situation in every quarter of the globe.
>
> I feel sure that the House will regard these results as highly satisfactory, and as reflecting the greatest credit upon the Admiralty and upon Admiral Cunningham, Commander-in-Chief in the Mediterranean, and, above all, on our pilots of the Fleet Air Arm, who, like their brothers in the Royal Air Force, continue to render the country services of the highest order.

This summed up the situation perfectly. At a crucial period in the battle for the Mediterranean, the strength of the Italian battle fleet had been halved. British morale at home was boosted, and the offensive spirit of the Italian naval high

command was undermined. This accounts for the poor performance of the Italian battle fleet at the battle of Cape Spartivento two weeks later, when Campioni had an excellent opportunity to inflict a defeat on Somerville's outnumbered Force H. Instead the Italian fleet withdrew, as Campioni had strict instructions not to risk what remained of his battleship force. The Italian press had demanded a victory, to demonstrate the fleet's morale and offensive spirit were intact after Taranto, but when this was denied them Campioni was relieved of his command.

On 10 January 1941 *Illustrious* was attacked by Fliegerkorps X, and was hit six times. The most serious damage was caused by a bomb, which penetrated the after lift and exploded inside the hangar. This photograph shows the after flight deck of *Illustrious* after the attack, which claimed the lives of 126 of its crew. *Illustrious* survived, and eventually limped into Malta's Grand Harbour.

There should have been other scapegoats. The Italian Air Force had failed to locate *Illustrious*, and allowed it to close within striking range of Taranto. This failure was due to a number of factors, including the lack of suitable aircraft, a lack of maritime reconnaissance training and a poor degree of cooperation between the Italian Navy and Air Force. It was also due to the presence of *Illustrious*' own fighters, who shielded their carrier from enemy aircraft. The Italian Air Force was also criticized for not avenging the attack by sinking *Illustrious* after the battle. This is unfair. It had to find it first, and on the morning of 12 November two or three Cant Z.01 'Gabbiano' flying boats were shot down by the carrier's Fulmar fighters as they tried to locate the British ship. A combination of radar warning and skilfully flown fighter cover created a barrier the Italian Air Force was unable to penetrate.

One more significant outcome of the attack was the decision by Nazi Germany that the Italians were no longer capable of winning the war in the Mediterranean without some help. This led to the almost immediate deployment of Fliegerkorps X (10th Air Corps) to the Mediterranean theatre. This air armada initially consisted of 80 Ju-88 'Stuka' dive-bombers, 92

The battleship *Littorio* was raised and repaired; it rejoined the Italian fleet in April 1941. In late July 1943 it was renamed *Italia*, and in September 1943 it surrendered to the Allies, following the Italian armistice. This photograph shows how the battleship appeared during 1942–43, when it was based in Taranto.

Ju-88 medium bombers, 27 He-111 torpedo bombers and 38 BF-110 fighters. It was therefore the Germans rather than the Italians who came close to avenging Taranto, when on 10 January *Illustrious* was attacked between Sicily and Tunisia by 63 German torpedo and dive-bombers, escorted by ten fighters. It was hit five times. One bomb failed to explode, but another struck its after lift, destroying 15 aircraft in its hangar. Nine of these were veterans of Taranto. *Illustrious* limped into Malta, and it was eventually repaired in the United States, and rejoined the fleet in early 1942. Fliegerkorps X continued to play a prominent part in the battle of the Mediterranean until the summer of 1943.

The attack on Taranto was the first raid of its kind. There has been much speculation over the influence the attack had on the Imperial Japanese Navy, and on the planning of its own much bigger attack on a naval base at Pearl Harbor. It is worth noting that soon after the raid, Lieutenant Commander Naito, the Japanese naval attaché in Berlin, was sent to Italy, with instructions to visit Taranto and report what he could about the way the attack was carried out. This report was duly passed to Admiral Yamamoto for evaluation. At the time Yamamoto was the commander of the Japanese Combined Fleet, and the architect of the plan to attack Pearl Harbor. Also, on his return to Japan, Naito personally briefed Commander Fuchida on the Taranto raid. Fuchida would go on to lead the attack on Pearl Harbor.

Then, in May 1941, a Japanese military and naval delegation toured Italy, and paid a visit to Ammiraglio di Squadra Iachino on his flagship *Littorio*, which had only just rejoined the fleet. During their visit, the members of the Japanese delegation asked numerous questions about the attack, and interviewed as many eyewitnesses as they could. The conclusion is that the Japanese were well aware of Operation *Judgement* and how it was carried out. However, the degree to which the attack on Taranto influenced the planning of the attack on Pearl Harbor is still a matter for debate. The big difference between the two attacks, of course, was one of scale. At Taranto the Fleet Air Arm carried out their attack using 20 biplanes. In December 1941 the Imperial Japanese Navy attacked Pearl Harbor using 353 modern naval aircraft – a mixture of fighters, dive-bombers and torpedo bombers.

This, though, did nothing to tarnish the achievement of 'Taranto Night'. Operation *Judgement* was a great success for the Fleet Air Arm – a victory the service still celebrates today. This success was achieved through meticulous planning, skilled reconnaissance and intelligence gathering, and made the best possible use of the arguably obsolete aircraft available to the Royal Navy. Thanks to Admiral Cunningham the operation was skilfully interwoven into a larger-scale naval campaign that helped disguise the bringing of *Illustrious* within striking range of Taranto. Above all, the attack on Taranto succeeded thanks to the skill, training and raw courage of the 40 young naval aviators who flew on the raid. Between them, they ushered in a new era in naval warfare.

Taranto has been described as the blueprint for Pearl Harbor, pictured here during the Japanese carrier-borne attack on the US Pacific Fleet on 7 December 1941. However, the Pearl Harbor attack was a far larger operation than the Taranto raid, carried out by almost 20 times the number of aircraft. Nevertheless, the Japanese planners were fully aware of what happened at Taranto, and just how effective the raid had been.

TARANTO TODAY

Just as it was in November 1940, Taranto is a naval port, as important to the Italian Navy as Portsmouth to the British or Newport News to the American fleets. It is also a bustling commercial port, administered by its own port authority, where container ships and other cargo vessels now sail through the waters once reserved for the Italian battle fleet. While the geography and general layout of the city and the harbour has not changed since 1940, the rapid expansion of this commercial port during the past 40 years has led to significant alterations in the layout of the anchorage. A large container terminal now lies to the west of the Mar Grande, just beyond Punta Rondinella, while behind it lies a vast petrochemical plant – the largest in Italy. It was over this stretch of coast that many of the Swordfish made their approach to the Mar Grande.

A more recognizable landmark is the curving line of the submerged breakwaters and the small islands that lie between the Mar Grande and the Gulf of Taranto. The small island of San Paolo is a designated military area, where the remains of the port's wartime defences can still be seen. Unfortunately these remains are of coastal batteries, rather than the anti-aircraft gun positions which defended the harbour in November 1940. The larger island of San Pietro is more informative. This low, wooded island has been left largely untouched since the war. Two anti-aircraft batteries stood here in 1940, on the north-eastern and south-eastern corners of the island. While no trace could be found of one of them, traces can still be seen of the north-eastern battery.

The main commercial port of Taranto lies to the north of the Mar Grande, and to the west of the city. Unfortunately modern developments seem to have removed any trace of the battery there, or those farther to the east, protecting the city and the canal leading to the Mar Piccolo. The canal is still there, guarded by the Castello Aragonese, the 15th-century stronghold, which guarded both the inner harbour and the city. It served as the port headquarters in 1940, and is still owned and run by the Italian Navy, which permits public access

Today, Taranto is a bustling commercial port, but it is also still a naval base, and the basic geography of the harbour is largely the same as it was during the war. Here, fishing boats lie in front of the historic centre (*centro storico*), the narrow streets of which have changed little for centuries. It was over this waterfront that many of the attackers approached the battleship anchorage in November 1940.

and provides tours. Unfortunately, while the castle's history is interpreted, there is little there relating to its use in 1940. Beyond it is the Ponte Girevole, the 19th-century swing bridge across the canal, which still operates much as it did in 1940, to permit the transit of warships and small commercial vessels through the canal.

To the east lies the old heart of Taranto, and the Tarantas, the palm-lined quayside, which lies at the southern shore of the Mar Piccolo. It is much as it was in 1940 – in fact it still forms part of the Marina Militare – the Naval Harbour – where vessels of the modern Italian Navy berth in the same 'Mediterranean mooring' fashion – stern facing the quayside – as their predecessors did in November 1940. It was this quayside – or rather the ships lining it – that was the principal target of the bomb-armed Swordfish in November 1940. While the restricted access of the naval harbour prevents public access, and a line of trees screens it from the rest of the city, the Tarantas can be visited by prior agreement with the Italian Navy, or during one of its regular open-day events.

The most evocative part of Taranto is the Mar Grande. Its full extent can be seen from the Palazzo Governo, or the long tree-lined Lungomare Vittorio Emanuele III, which runs along the edge of the water. It was to the south of this spot, between it and the Diga di Tarantola breakwater, that the Italian battleships lay at anchor on the evening of 11 November 1940. A little farther down the coast, just past a small yacht marina, is the foreshore where the *Caio Duilio* was beached after the raid. The rather ugly waterfront area to the south – between the marina and the main naval base – provides limited access to the water, but it was in front of here that the *Littorio* was torpedoed. The naval base is strictly off limits, and its layout has changed since 1940, but essentially it is the same dockyard that served the Regia Marina, and from where tugs and auxiliary vessels were ordered to help save the three stricken battleships. It is off here that the *Conti di Cavour* was torpedoed, and where it was beached close to the refuelling pier, which is still in use today. Farther to the south the end of the Diga di Tarantola – once protected by barrage balloons – can still be accessed by a road serving another yacht marina and warehouse area.

From the southern waterfront of Taranto a visitor can still enjoy an uninterrupted view over the Mar Grande. Here, a small breakwater lies in front of the historic centre (*centro storico*), near the Molo Sant Eligio, in the north-west corner of the outer harbour. In the distance lies the modern commercial port, on the western side of the city.

Farther inland, the oil storage depot bombed by the flare droppers is still there, dwarfed by the more modern sewage treatment plant that serves the city and its environs. Farther to the north the Ponte Aldo Moro cuts the Mar Piccolo in two. To the east of the bridge, on the inner harbour's southern shore, is the site of the seaplane base which was bombed during the raid. This area, too, is part of a protected military area, and is off limits to casual visitors. However, from the sea, the seaplane

A modern Italian patrol boat transits the Canale Navigabile, which links the Mar Piccolo and the Mar Grande. It has just passed through the Ponte Girevoli swing bridge, while on the left is the Castello Aragonese, which protects the seaward side of the city. Behind the warship is the Mar Piccolo, with its naval dockyard and quayside, which is out of view to the right in this photograph.

slipways can still be seen, although modern warehouses now stand on the site once occupied by the base itself. While overall, the presence of restricted areas means that a visitor will be unable to visit all of the sites relevant to the attack on Taranto, enough remains to give a good overall impression of the harbour, its geography and its defences. It takes little to imagine what the same vistas would have looked like on the night of 11–12 November 1940.

FURTHER READING

Bragadin, Marc, *The Italian Navy in World War II* (Annapolis, 1956) US Naval Institute Press

Brescia, Maurizio, *Mussolini's Navy: A Reference Guide to the Regia Marina, 1930–1945* (Barnsley, 2012) Seaforth Publishing

Chesneau, Roger, *Aircraft Carriers of the World, 1914 to Present: An Illustrated Encyclopaedia* (London, 1992) Arms & Armour Press

Gardiner, Robert, *Conway's All the World's Fighting Ships, 1922–1946* (London, 1980) Conway Maritime Press

Greene, Jack & Massignani, Alessandro, *The Naval War in the Mediterranean, 1940–43* (Rochester, 1998) Chatham Publishing

Lamb, Charles, *To War in a Stringbag* (London, 1980) Bantam Books

Lowry, Thomas P., *The Attack on Taranto: Blueprint for Pearl Harbor* (London, 2001) Stackpole Books

Newton, Don & Hampshire, Cecil, *Taranto* (London, 1959) New English Library

Roskill, Capt. S. W., *The War at Sea, 1939–45* (London, 1960) HMSO [Vol. I]

Schofield, Vice-Admiral B. B., *Stringbags in Action: Taranto 1940 & Bismarck 1941* (Barnsley, 1988) Pen & Sword

Smith, Peter C., *Critical Conflict: The Royal Navy's Mediterranean Campaign in 1940* (Barnsley, 2011) Pen & Sword

Smithers, A. J., *Taranto 1940: A Glorious Episode* (London, 1995) Leo Cooper

Stephen, Martin, *Sea Battles in Close-Up: World War 2* (London, 1988) Ian Allen Ltd

Wellham, John, *With Naval Wings: An Autobiography of a Fleet Air Arm Pilot in World War II* (London, 2007) Spellmount

Whitley, M. J., *Battleships of World War Two: An International Encyclopaedia* (London, 1998) Arms & Armour Press

Winton, John, *Air Power at Sea, 1939–45* (London, 1976) Sedgwick & Jackson

Wragg, David, *The Fleet Air Arm Handbook, 1939–45* (Stroud, 2001) Sutton

Wragg, David, *Stringbag: The Fairey Swordfish at War* (Barnsley, 2004) Pen & Sword

Wragg, David, *Swordfish: the Story of the Taranto Raid* (London, 2003) Weidenfeld & Nicolson

INDEX